Praise for *The John Carlos Story*

"*The John Carlos Story* is the remarkable chronicle of an epic life sketched against the defining crisis of race in America. Carlos's athletic genius on the field is matched by his heroic will to overcome trials and tribulations in his personal life, and to find resurrection in his professional life. This is an inspiring and eloquent story about a great American whose commitment to truth, justice, and democracy were tested and found true."

—Michael Eric Dyson, author, *Can You Hear Me Now?*

"John Carlos's life story is an insightful and gripping look at the times he lived and the Olympics he helped make so memorable. He shows us that the one day that made him famous was only the most outward and visible sign of a touching and thoughtful life."

—Frank Deford, author, *Bliss, Remembered*

"In this breathlessly readable tale, John Carlos finally steps out of that iconic photograph to become the vibrant, fascinating hero we never really knew."

—Robert Lipsyte, author, *An Accidental Sportswriter*

"John Carlos tells a compelling story of courage and the consequences of action. He, Tommie Smith, and many other black athletes took a stand against racial injustice in the United States and racial injustice in sports. They were ridiculed by many mainstream commentators at the time, but their actions helped to transform both the sports world and this country. This book is by and about someone who has been and remains one of my heroes."

—Bill Fletcher Jr., editorial board member, *The Black Commentator*

"John Carlos was a principal in creating the most iconic sports image of the twentieth century, the demonstration for racial equality and justice from the victory stand at the 1968 Mexico City Olympics. The background and evolution of his perspectives and politics from the vantage point of forty-plus years later is illuminating, inspirational, provocative, and very much worth the read."

—Harry Edwards, professor emeritus, University of California, Berkeley, and organizer, 1968 Olympic Project for Human Rights

"John Carlos's story of bravery and sacrifice will warm your heart. But beyond his individual heroism, it speaks to the power of athletes who bodaciously refuse to just 'shut up and play.' Carlos and Zirin capture the way that through sports, the actions of a few athletes resonate across the globe."

—**William Hunter, executive director, National Basketball Players Association**

"If a picture is worth one thousand words, then the defiant image of John Carlos and Tommie Smith, with their clenched black-gloved fists raised high in protest at the 1968 Olympics, must be worth at least one thousand more. In *The John Carlos Story*, one of those icons from '68 uses his own words to describe that picture and a lifetime of substance that ultimately transcends such a famous moment in time. Providing context to history, *The John Carlos Story* rocks with the soulful energy of Black Power in this modern time."

—**Dr. Todd Boyd, author, media commentator, and the Katherine and Frank Price Endowed Chair for the Study of Race and Popular Culture at the USC School of Cinematic Arts**

"History tells us iconic moments in sports are always enveloped in personal stories of sacrifice, courage, and angst. The lasting images that we see occur in a flash contain enriching back stories that are typically even more significant and tragic than the moment itself. John Carlos and Dave Zirin have combined to tell such a story. The moment that two men stood on the world platform to take a stand after they had become the best in the world is rich, complicated, and, most important, as relevant today as it was in Mexico City. [John Carlos and Dave Zirin] bring out a beautiful and passionate voice of truth to readers in this book about a man who became a legend."

—**DeMaurice Smith, Director NFL Players Assiciation**

"*The John Carlos Story* is a blow-by-blow detailing of triumph versus tragedy from the jump. Again Dave Zirin uncovers and illuminates the mere footnotes of this sports history hero with his impeccable balance of truth. This story drills a hole into the myth of black athlete success and worship."

—**Chuck D, Public Enemy**

The John Carlos Story

The Sports Moment That Changed the World

■　■　■　■

John Carlos
with Dave Zirin

Haymarket Books
Chicago, Illinois

First published in 2011 by
Haymarket Books
P.O. Box 180165
Chicago, IL 60618
773-583-7884
www.haymarketbooks.org
info@haymarketbooks.org

ISBN: 978-1-60846-127-1

Trade distribution:
In the US, Consortium Book Sales and Distribution, www.cbsd.com
In Canada, Publishers Group Canada, www.pgcbooks.ca
In the UK, Turnaround Publisher Services, www.turnaround-uk.com
In Australia, Palgrave Macmillan, www.palgravemacmillan.com.au
All other countries, Publishers Group Worldwide, www.pgw.com

Cover design by Russell Robinson. Cover image of John Carlos raising his fist in
a Black Power salute on the Olympic podium after winning a bronze medal in the
1968 Olympic Games in Mexico City (Associated Press).

This book was published with the generous support
of Lannan Foundation and the Wallace Global Fund.

Printed in the United States.

Library of Congress Cataloging-in-Publication data is available.

3 5 7 9 10 8 6 4 2

Contents

First and foremost, all praise to God, the Almighty

To my wife Charlene, my father, Earl, my mother, Vioris, all my brothers and sisters—Earl Jr., Mark, and Hepsey—and especially to my brother Andrew who left this world too soon on March 13, 2011. This book would have meant so much to him

To my beautiful children, Kimme, Travian, Malik, Shanna, and Winsetta, who were strongest when times were toughest

To my friends and associates Blaine Robinson, Dwane Tillman, and C. D. Jackson

To Dave Cunningham, George Foreman, Tommie Smith, Lee Evans, Wyomia Tyus, and every member of the 1968 Olympic Team

Thank you so much to the beloved principal at Palm Springs High School, Ricky Wright

With all my love and sincerity, to those regular folks around the world fighting for justice from the Midwest of the United States to the Middle East. All they want is what we wanted forty-three years ago: dignity and an acknowledgment of our humanity

Foreword

■   ■   ■   ■

Cornel West

John Carlos is one of the grand figures of the twentieth century. His incredible political courage, indisputable athletic excellence, and indestructible spiritual fortitude sets him apart from most contemporary celebrities. In fact, his fame derives from his courage, excellence, and fortitude. Yet it is only in this powerful and poignant memoir that we learn of what he is made and who made him that way.

John Carlos is the human extension of a great family, great community, and great movement. Earl Vanderbilt Carlos and Vioris Carlos gave birth to John on June 5, 1945. His father, born in Camden, South Carolina, was a strong and proud black man in Jim Crow America. His mother, born in Jamaica and raised in Cuba, was a beautiful and determined woman in Jane Crow America. John was Harlem born and Harlem raised—a native son of the Big Apple. Even as a youth, he was on fire for justice—from his Robin Hood disposition to his precious moments spent with Malcolm X. He was known in the neighborhood for taking a stand for the vulnerable.

Like most young black men, John Carlos directed his energy and talent toward sports and entertainment. He excelled in swimming—winning the New York City 200-meter freestyle championships. And he spent time with the legendary Fred Astaire in front of the famous Savoy Ballroom. Yet ugly racism turned him away from swimming to track and field. And he always retained his love of flair. His dyslexia was a major impediment for academic excellence—yet his quest for wisdom is genuine and endless.

John Carlos's decision to attend East Texas State was a pivotal moment in his life. Commerce, Texas, was light-years away from Harlem, USA. And relocating his precious family to Jim Crow Texas was even more adventurous. Yet they triumphed. John Carlos's record-setting performances on the track led him to the historic Olympic Project for Human Rights—the attempt of black athletes to boycott the 1968 Olympics in Mexico City. Working alongside Lee Evans, Tommie Smith, and Dr. Harry Edwards, Carlos joined the athletic wing of the black freedom movement. His meeting with Martin Luther King Jr. in New York City in support of the boycott is a lovely story. Needless to say, the buildup to Mexico City, the race, the unforgettable protest (gestures and symbolic socks, gloves, and beads), the solidarity with Mexican students, the deep bond with the Australian athlete Peter Norman, and the vicious treatment after the protest are the heart of this fascinating memoir.

The majestic spirit of John Carlos looms large in the darkness he encounters after Mexico City. He struggles, he suffers, and he shudders. Yet he endures with dignity—along with the help of family, especially Charlene, and friends like Rosie Grier and Mayor Tom Bradley. This courageous memoir is a testament to the triumph of John Carlos in the face of terror, trauma, and stigma. It is the tale of a strong black man who overcame forces trying to crush him—still on fire for justice and with a smile on his face!

Preface

■ ■ ■ ■

Dave Zirin

It was inevitable that this revolt of the black athlete should develop.
With struggles being waged by black people in the areas of education,
housing, employment, and many others, it was only a matter of time
before Afro-American athletes shed their fantasies and delusions and
asserted their manhood and faced the facts of their existence.
—Dr. Harry Edwards, organizer, Olympic Project for Human Rights

It has been almost forty-three years since Tommie Smith, the son of a migrant worker, and Harlem's John Carlos took the medal stand in the 200-meter dash at the 1968 Olympics and created what must be considered the most enduring, riveting image in the history of either sports or protest. But while the image has stood the test of time, the struggle that led to that moment has been cast aside, a casualty of our culture of political amnesia.

Smith and Carlos's gesture of resistance was not the result of some spontaneous urge to get face time on the evening news or any desire to boost their profile. It was instead a product of the revolt of black athletes in the 1960s. In the fall of 1967, amateur black athletes formed OPHR, the Olympic Project for Human Rights, to organize an African American boycott of the 1968 Olympics in Mexico City. OPHR, its lead organizer, Dr. Harry Edwards, and its primary athletic spokespeople, Smith and 400-meter sprinter Lee Evans, were deeply influenced by the black freedom struggle. Their goal was nothing less than to expose how the United States used black athletes to project a lie about race relations both at home and internationally.

In their founding statement, they wrote,

> We must no longer allow this country to use a few so-called Negroes to point out to the world how much progress she has made in solving her racial problems when the oppression of Afro-Americans is greater than it ever was. We must no longer allow the sports world to pat itself on the back as a citadel of racial justice when the racial injustices of the sports world are infamously legendary . . . any black person who allows himself to be used in the above matter is a traitor because he allows racist whites the luxury of resting assured that those black people in the ghettos are there because that is where they want to be. So we ask why should we run in Mexico only to crawl home?

OPHR had four central demands: hire more Black coaches, restore Muhammad Ali's heavyweight boxing title, remove Avery Brundage as head of the International Olympic Committee (IOC), and disinvite South Africa and Rhodesia from the Olympics. Ali's belt had been taken by the boxing powers that be earlier in the year for his resistance to the Vietnam draft. By standing with Ali, OPHR was expressing its opposition to the war. By calling for the ouster of IOC head Avery Brundage, they were dragging out of the shadows a part of Olympic history those in power wanted to bury. Brundage was an anti-Semite and a white supremacist, best remembered today for sealing the deal on Hitler's hosting of the 1936 Olympics in Berlin. By demanding the exclusion of South Africa and Rhodesia, they aimed to convey their internationalism and solidarity with the black freedom struggles against apartheid in Africa.

The wind went out of the sails of a broader boycott for many reasons, most centrally because the IOC recommitted to banning South Africa from the games. But as John Carlos makes clear in this book, there were other even more pressing reasons. Athletes who had spent their whole lives preparing for their Olympic moment simply didn't want to give it up. They couldn't agree that the Olympics should be a stage of struggle, not when the sacrifice could be so great as the loss of the opportunity to compete on a world stage after years of predawn training sessions.

There also emerged accusations of a campaign of harassment and intimidation orchestrated by people supportive of Brundage. Although nothing was ever proven, fear of retribution from the Olympic establishment certainly helped to undermine the boycott. Despite these pressures, a handful of black Olympians was still determined to make a stand. Across the globe, they were hardly alone.

The atmosphere in the lead-up to the Olympics in Mexico City was electric with struggle. Already in 1968, the world had seen the Tet Offensive in Vietnam, proving that the US military was mired in a crisis far worse than generals, politicians, and the press had heretofore revealed. The Prague Spring, during which Czech students challenged tanks from the Stalinist Soviet Union, demonstrated that dissent was crackling on both sides of the Iron Curtain. The April 4 assassination of Martin Luther King Jr. and the urban uprisings that followed—along with the exponential growth of the Black Panther Party in the United States—revealed an African American freedom struggle unassuaged by the civil rights reforms that had transformed the Jim Crow South. In France, the largest general strike in world history demonstrated unprecedented alliances between workers and students. Then, on October 2, ten days before the opening ceremonies of the 1968 Olympic Games, Mexican security forces massacred hundreds of students and workers in Mexico City's Tlatelolco Square.

Although the harassment and intimidation of the OPHR athletes cannot be compared to this slaughter, the intention was the same—to stifle protest and make sure that the Olympics were "suitable" for visiting dignitaries, heads of state, and an international audience. It was not successful.

As the time for the 200-meter dash approached, IOC officials fretted that OPHR athletes might succeed in giving expression to the global spirit of resistance that the IOC had hoped to keep from intruding on the "sanctity" of the Olympic spectacle. Brundage took the step of sending track and field legend Jesse Owens to the Olympic locker room to discourage any protest.

Jesse Owens was the most remarkable athlete of his time. On September 12, 1913, James Cleveland Owens was born the son of sharecroppers who toiled in the fields of Oakville, Alabama. The lack of even basic health care meant that Owens lost several siblings to early death, and he had his own brush with mortality when his mother had to cut a fibrous tumor out of his chest with a kitchen knife. But Owens loved to run, and he found glory when he won four gold medals at the 1936 Olympics in Hitler's Germany and dealt a humiliating blow to Nazi theories of racial superiority.

But despite all of Owens's accomplishments, he could not outrun the reality of what it meant to be a black man in 1936 upon returning home. Opportunities were scarce, even for a college graduate with four gold medals. By December 1936, he was racing Julio McCaw, a five-year-old horse, in a sideshow spectacle to put food on the table. But after years outside Brundage's Olympic industry, Owens was brought back into the fold to serve the purpose of discouraging a new generation of track radicals.

As sports sociologist Douglas Hartmann wrote in his book *Race, Culture and the Revolt of the Black Athlete: The 1968 Olympic Protests,* "In Owens's view, the boycott was nothing but 'political aggrandizement,' which he condemned on the grounds that 'there is no place in the athletic world for politics.' Instead, Owens claimed, 'The Olympics help bridge the gap of misunderstanding of people in this country,' thus promoting 'the way of American life.' In a follow-up statement published under the title 'Olympics a Bastion of Non-Discrimination,' the legendary figure added that athletic scholarships help youngsters to attend the colleges of their choice."

As 1968 Olympian Lee Evans told me,

Jesse was confused as far as I'm concerned. The USOC dogged him, and he knew they dogged him. Treating him badly after his exploits in the Olympic games. . . . We were really annoyed with him because he knew what we were going through, yet he pretended that it didn't exist and that just blew our minds when he called a meeting with us in Mexico City. I thought he called this meeting because Avery Brundage sent him there. Jesse Owens was sitting on the fifty-yard line with all the important people of the world, the royalties, the Avery Brundages. They have a special section where they sit in the games right at the fifty-yard line and Jesse, that's where he was sitting. He thought he was one of them. He had forgot that he was once an athlete struggling like we were. So he came and talked to us like he was Avery Brundage or the King of England or somebody and really talking stupid to us and we just shouted him out of the room. And then out of the blue he said, "You know, wearing those long black socks [running socks that were an act of identification with the black freedom struggle] is going to cut off the circulation in your legs." That's what he told us. We said this guy is really out of his mind! This is when we ran him out of there. I still admire him to this day, that's why I say he was confused, coming to talk to us like that because we knew that he was being victimized. He was a victim, and we felt sorry for him actually.

Owens said to Smith and Carlos, "The black fist is a meaningless symbol. When you open it, you have nothing but fingers—weak, empty fingers. The only time the black fist has significance is when there's money inside. There's where the power lies."

Owens's words to Smith and Carlos that day backfired. On the second day of the games, Smith and Carlos took their stand. Smith set a world record, winning the 200-meter gold, and Carlos captured the bronze. Smith then took out the black gloves. The silver medalist, a runner from Australia named Peter Norman, attached an OPHR patch onto his chest to show his solidarity on the medal stand. (Norman was far more than just a bystander and also paid a terrific price for his act of solidarity.)

As the stars and stripes ran up the flagpole and the national anthem played, Smith and Carlos bowed their heads and raised their fists in what was described across the globe as a "Black Power salute," creating a moment that would define, for better and worse, the rest of their lives. But there was far more to their actions on the medal stand than just the gloves. The two men wore no shoes, to protest black poverty. They wore beads around their necks, to protest lynching.

Within hours, word was out that Smith and Carlos had been stripped of their medals (although this was not in fact true) and expelled from the Olympic Village. Avery Brundage justified this by saying, assumedly with a straight face, "They violated one of the basic principles of the Olympic games: that politics play no part whatsoever in them."

Ironically, it was Brundage's reaction that really spurred the protest and catapulted it into the limelight. As the preeminent sportswriter of the century, Red Smith, wrote, "By throwing a fit over the incident, suspending the young men and ordering them out of Mexico, [Brundage] multiplied the impact of the protest a hundredfold."

In Brundage's unpublished autobiography written years later, he was still muttering about Smith and Carlos. "Warped mentalities and cracked personalities seem to be everywhere and impossible to eliminate," he wrote.

But Brundage was not alone in his furious reaction. The *Los Angeles Times* accused Smith and Carlos of a "Nazi-like salute." *Time* had a distorted version of the Olympic logo on its cover, but instead of the motto "Faster, Higher, Stronger," blared "Angrier, Nastier, Uglier." The *Chicago Tribune* called the act "an embarrassment visited upon the country," an "act contemptuous of the United States," and "an insult to their countrymen." Smith and Carlos were "renegades" who would come home to be "greeted as heroes by fellow extremists," lamented the paper.

But the coup de grâce was delivered by a young reporter for the *Chicago American* named Brent Musburger. "One gets a little tired of having the United States run down by athletes who are enjoying themselves at the expense of their country," he wrote. "Protesting and working constructively against racism in the United States is one thing, but airing one's dirty clothing before the entire world during a fun-and-games tournament was no more than a juvenile gesture by a couple of athletes who should have known better." He then described Smith and Carlos as "a pair of black-skinned storm troopers." The remarks from Musburger, who was soon catapulted to national network fame, scarred and infuriate Carlos to this day.

The harshest rebuke came from fellow Olympian and boxer George Foreman, who upon winning the gold medal, waved a miniature American flag and bowed to the Mexico City audience. This was perceived by many as an act of anti-solidarity with Smith and Carlos. As damaging as that moment was, it could have been worse. As Carlos explains in these pages, he and Smith narrowly missed being there in the front row for Foreman's display of support for the Olympic "tradition."

But if Smith and Carlos were attacked from a multitude of directions, they also received many expressions of support, including from some unlikely sources. For example, the US Olympic crew team, all white and entirely from Harvard, issued the following statement: "We—as individuals—have been concerned about the place of the black man in American society in their struggle for equal rights. As members of the U.S. Olympic team, each of us has come to feel a moral commitment to support our black teammates in their efforts to dramatize the injustices and inequities which permeate our society."

OPHR and the actions of Smith and Carlos were a stunning rebuke to the hypocrisy at the heart of the Olympics. Brundage's Olympics professed to be about athletics over politics and a venue that brought nations together. But in reality, it was an orgy of nationalism resting on a foundation of politics that excused and legitimized apartheid nations and fascist dictators.

Unfortunately, the OPHR also mirrored a deep flaw found in other sections of the New Left and Black Power movements: women were largely shut out. Many of OPHR's calls to action had statements about "reclaiming manhood," as if African American women weren't victims of racism or couldn't be part of a strong movement against it. Despite this exclusion, many women athletes eventually became major voices of solidarity. "I'd like to say that we dedicate our relay win to John Carlos and Tommie Smith," said Wyomia Tyus, the anchor of the women's gold-medal-winning 4x100 relay team.

Smith and Carlos's display on the medal stand was a watershed moment of resistance. It has been enshrined in the national consciousness and immortalized in popular culture—from Reebok ads with P-Diddy adopting the Smith and Carlos pose to an appearance on *The Simpsons*. Unlike other 1960s iconography—Woodstock, Abbie Hoffman, Richard Nixon—the moment doesn't feel musty. It still packs a wallop. In Harlem, street-corner merchants even today sell T-shirts with the image of Smith and Carlos emblazoned on them. On HBO in the fall of 2010, you could watch the 2004 documentary *Fists of Freedom*, which told the story behind the protest. On ESPN, a frequent question posed to athletes competing in the 2008 Games in Beijing was whether they would "pull a Smith and Carlos" to protest the lack of human rights in China—though the question is somewhat off the mark since the two former athletes did not go to Mexico City to criticize Mexico. In 2010, I appeared on a panel on the history of sports and resistance with Carlos, after which a long line of young people born years—even decades—after 1968 patiently waited for his signature on everything from posters and T-shirts to hastily procured pieces of notebook paper.

Why has that moment over forty years ago retained its cultural capital? The most obvious is that people love a good redemption song. Smith and Carlos have been proven correct. They were reviled for taking a stand and using the Olympic podium to do it. But their "radical" demands have since proved to be prescient. Today the idea of standing up to apartheid South Africa, racism, and for Muhammad Ali seems a matter of common decency rather than radical rabble-rousing. After years of death threats and being treated as pariahs in the world of athletics, Smith and Carlos attend ceremonial unveilings of statues erected in their honor. It's a remarkable journey that says volumes about how new generations have come to appreciate their struggle and sacrifice.

There's another reason why the image of black-gloved fists thrust in the air have retained their power. Smith and Carlos sacrificed privilege and glory, fame and fortune, for a larger cause—civil rights. As Carlos says, "A lot of the [black] athletes thought that winning [Olympic] medals would supercede or protect them from racism. But even if you won a medal, it ain't going to save your momma. It ain't going to save your sister or children. It might give you fifteen minutes of fame, but what about the rest of your life?"

Carlos's attitude resonates because we still live in a world where racism is evident. If Hurricane Katrina taught us nothing else, it's that for every Barack Obama and Condoleezza Rice, there are many communities from New Orleans to South Central Los Angeles where poverty on one side and racism on the other form a vice that crushes the potential of too many black Americans.

We are constantly told that "sports and politics don't mix." The great Howard Cosell, in a venomous critique, once said that this was "rule number 1 of the Jockocracy." The supposedly pristine idealism of sports, of competition on an equal playing field, was to be quarantined from that nasty political netherworld where ideas and social concerns threatened to ruin the party.

Today, major sports columnists deliver a flurry of verbal body blows to any athlete who dares to take a political stand. But in an era when the building of publicly funded stadiums has become a substitute for anything resembling an urban policy; at a time when local governments build public stadiums on the taxpayers' dime, siphoning off millions of dollars into commercial enterprises even as schools, hospitals, and bridges crumble, one can hardly say that sports exists in a world completely distinct from political concerns. When the sports pages are filled with lurid tales of steroid use, high-profile sexual harassment suits, and endless speculation about the personal lives of players like Ben Roethlisberger and Tiger

Woods, then we've entered a realm of sports reporting as tabloid distraction instead of as a lens to better understand our world.

Critical is the understanding that sports can also be a place of inspiration that doesn't transcend the political but becomes the political, a place where we see our own dreams and aspirations played out in dynamic Technicolor. "Politics" can seem remote and alien to the vast majority of people. But the playing field is where we can project our every thought, fear, and hope. We want to believe fiercely that it is the one place where ability alone is how we are judged. If you *can* play, you *will* play—no matter your color, class, sex, or ethnicity. This is why boxers like Joe Louis and Muhammad Ali, Olympic stars like Wilma Rudolph and Jim Thorpe, tennis players like Billie Jean King and the Williams sisters, are viewed consciously or not as political beings, carriers of the dream that the playing field for all of us might be made a little more level. John Carlos is central to this tradition and this is why his story feels simultaneously relevant and revelatory. This is someone who was the first person in history to win the 100, 200, and 4x100 races in both the NCAA and NAIA finals. This is someone who stiff-armed a place in the athletic pantheon because he felt like he had something to say, even if it meant paying a hellacious price.

John Carlos's story—a heartbreaking, remarkably principled, and painful journey—holds the potential to bring strength to both civic-minded athletes and sports-minded citizens concerned by the pressing social issues of our times. But it's also more than that. John Carlos's family history is a story of migration, of struggling to make ends meet, of dreaming of a better life, of service in the armed forces, of fighting for democracy abroad and finding it lacking at home. It's a uniquely American story, one that deserves to be told for what it can teach us about the sacrifices made so the next generation can move forward.

Introduction

■　■　■　■

To Sleep with Anger

It's ESPN. Owned by Disney. An empire of its own. And they are flying me to Mexico City. They want to film Tommie Smith and me as we return to the infamous site of what they call "the fists of freedom." They had already given us an award at their awards show. The Arthur Ashe Courage Award, it was called. People stood and clapped for us. I just can't believe it. I'm no star, no hero. I'm a guidance counselor at Palm Springs High School in California. As recently as three years ago, I was lonelier than a raindrop in the Sahara. No one wanted to talk to me. No one wanted to say my name. Some young reporter found me in my office in California and asked if after all these years I felt embraced. "I don't feel embraced, I feel like a survivor, like I survived cancer," I told him. "It's like if you are sick and no one wants to be around you, and when you're well, everyone who thought you would go down for good doesn't even want to make eye contact. It was almost like we were on a deserted island. That's where Tommy Smith and John Carlos were. But we survived."

Then I was just a survivor and I was simply alone.

Now I'm waiting to get on this plane and go to Mexico City because people want to hear what I think. A man of African descent is about to walk into the Oval Office, and the cameras want to record a story about the progress made by black people and how far we've come. If they want to hear that story, they're talking to the wrong man. I have a story. You better believe I have a story. But it's not that story.

It starts by understanding what is happening to me right now. No, not getting on this plane to Mexico City. Right now, a young man is staring at me, smiling. He comes up to me, a little scruff of beard on his chin, a twinkle in his eye and a half smile. No *hello*. No *how are you*. I know what's coming next because it happens too many times to count. He throws his fist in the air, bows his head, and says, "I just had to do that." Then he scampers off. No autograph request. No "Hello, Mr. Carlos." No goodbyes. My friend asks me if that happens often. I try—and fail—to look annoyed, but I can't hide the crinkle at the corners of my mouth. I say, "Every damn day"—and at that moment—for just a second—my knee doesn't feel like someone took a sledgehammer to it, courtesy of a Philadelphia Eagles training camp many years ago (I'll get to that part of the story later). My eyes don't sting with infections. My kidneys don't feel like I just went fifteen rounds with Rocky Balboa. I am twenty-two again. And I feel a joyous sense of a life well lived.

Because here is the secret: I still feel the fire. It's been forty years, but if I shut my eyes, I can still feel the fire from those days, and if I open my eyes, I still see the fires all around me. I didn't like the way the world *was*, and I believe that there needs to be some changes about the way the world *is*. I'm still feeling the fire about the way history can take these sacred moments of struggle and sell them back to us by the pound. I feel the fire about the way my heroes Malcolm X and Paul Robeson have become postage stamps. I feel the fire that Muhammad Ali has become a walking postage stamp, a man without a voice. I feel the fire that Dr. King is a commemorative cup at McDonald's. I'm angry that all our political teeth have been subjected to a pop culture root canal.

Let's start with that phrase defining who we were: "The Revolt of the Black Athlete." You can take that to the cleaners right now. It's a way of keeping us on the playing field, safe, sweet, and sellable. I don't think of it as the revolt of the black athlete at all. It was the revolt of the black man. Athletics was my occupation. I didn't do what I did as an athlete. I raised my voice in protest as a man. I was fortunate to grow up in the era of Dr. King and Paul Robeson, of baseball players like Jackie Robinson and Roy Campanella. Roy used to come into my dad's shoe-repair shop on 142nd Street and Lenox in Harlem. I could see how they were treated as black athletes. I would ask myself, "Why is this happening?" Racism meant that none of us could truly have our day in the sun. Without education, housing, and employment, we were going down the drain—from "family hood" to "neighborhood" to just "the hood." If you can't give your wife or son or daughter what they need to live, after a while you try to escape who you are. That's why people turn to drugs and why our communities have been destroyed. And that's why there was a revolt. That's also why I wrote this book. Not to tear anyone or anything down, but to rebuild.

One

■ ■ ■ ■

Harlem World

Harlem. Born and raised. I came to this earth on June 5, 1945. I was a breech birth, which meant that I arrived with my backside facing the world, making it that much more difficult for everyone around me. Funny that.

626 Lenox Avenue was my first address. It was roughly half a block from the Savoy Ballroom, maybe just another stone's throw to the Cotton Club. If you don't know the names of those two magical places, then you need to look them up. This was where you could find music, dance, and the finest performers of the twentieth century. Right in the heart of Harlem, where the days were rough, and the nights came alive as the swells came uptown because we were the home of the best. Growing up, it made me feel—to be so close to so much greatness—that I didn't have to sit on the back of anybody's bus.

Yes, I was there in the midst of the Harlem Renaissance. And then I watched it become a casualty, strangled in the crib, crying for the music that had stopped playing. Harlem back then is what I would call "salt and pepper." It was white folks, black folks, and a community of togetherness, at least to my young eyes. We were like a salad bowl, so to speak, at that particular time. The nation was segregated, Harlem was integrated. But then, just as we saw people marching down South for integration on our television screens, with the dogs and the hoses, I began to see this exodus. I was nine years old. The white folks decided to pack up and leave Harlem, and they took their savings with them.

You know what real estate costs in Harlem today? I bet they regret it now. But this process, called gentrification, comes at its own price. Way too much of Uptown has become off limits, as we've been just priced out. I am glad my old stomping grounds aren't a war zone anymore, but I feel like I can't go home again because my home is a memory.

Among my circle of friends, I was one of the fortunate kids because I had a mom and a dad in the household. The drug epidemic was just starting its slow burn in Harlem, and among too many members of my community, it hung around our necks like a noose on fire. There was "King Kong," which was like drinkable PCP. The drugs always had an easier path into single-parent homes. A lot of people lived their lives around drugs and alcohol until it crushed them. Fortunately for me, I had a mom, a dad, two brothers, and one sister who stayed clear of all the junk. Sometimes it felt like luck, sometimes it felt like someone was watching over us, and sometimes it just felt like we were all so focused on getting out, we stayed clear of what would have chained us to a sinking ship.

My father's name was Earl Vanderbilt Carlos. He was born in 1895, just thirty-two years after the Emancipation Proclamation, a sharecropper's son in Camden, South Carolina. He fought in the First World War, in which he won a whole series of citations for bravery in a segregated army. Ask him about the war and he'd tell you that the white officers treated him one way and one way only: "Like shit." By trade, he was a carpenter, but his skill set was with a pair of shoes. He was a man with a trade that today hardly exists and probably seems as remote and distant as being born in the nineteenth century and winning medals in the First World War. He was a cobbler, a shoemaker with his own shop, a slick combination of bunched muscles and nimble fingers. In my eyes, when he roamed that shop, he was a man of authority and a trade that stretched back in time. But on the side, he was no one's cobbler. "Big Earl" Carlos was a hustler and a gambler of the first order.

"Big Earl" made it clear, though, that the hustle was for after work and not a replacement for the hard labor that built the stability our family depended on in a neighborhood that could be a roller coaster of excitement and pitfalls.

My father was a workingman. He would open his storefront doors at seven o'clock in the morning and keep them open until eight at night sometimes. He treated his three young boys like men. He wanted to make sure we had freedom to do our thing and learn our way, but he was very stern about certain things, like going to school. He said, "You better put time in at that desk until the end of the day."

Then came the hustle.

That wasn't just my daddy. That was almost every black man in our neighborhood at that particular time. Black men, in particular, just couldn't make it off the salaries that they were earning at that particular time. They always had their little ballroom craps game going, or a poker game, or they were running the numbers, that kind of thing. And I remember when the poker game was at my house, my mom would sell dinners to folks gathered around the table. My father would stop the game, and every last person there would have to drop something in the till. And drop they would. Me and my brothers, Andrew and Earl Jr., would be serving drinks, bringing them food, whatever we could do. I saw a bunch of fellas talking, eating, smoking—and some with math skills in counting cards that would shame a professor at MIT. I think this is just a snapshot of a lot of families doing what they had to do to make ends meet.

My mom, Vioris, was born in Jamaica and raised in Cuba until she was seventeen. She was a nurse's aide at Bellevue Hospital in New York City. My mom worked days, and then she switched to the night shift so the small wages a nurse's aide brought home were just a pinch higher, but every pinch counted. For everyone out there who ever had a mom work nights—midnight to 8 a.m.—you know what that does to a family. You wake up with a bad dream, you're not going to wake up Earl Vanderbilt Carlos, so you miss your mother terribly. But at the same time, you are filled with a special kind of awe that someone would sacrifice so much for you, your brothers, and your sisters. A family can go one of two ways when the mother works such difficult hours: it can split you apart or bring you together. We stayed together. We stayed together because we saw it like we were all in the same boat and part of the same project. School was just one part of our lives. Everyone worked, and everyone hustled. My brothers and me worked in my father's shop. And I, along with my crew, opened the cab doors for the swells over at the Savoy Ballroom.

I always had my crew—five or six fellas who I still count among some of the best friends a person could ever have. We rolled together day and night, and we lived to hustle. How couldn't we? If you lived in Hershey, Pennsylvania, you'd probably dig on chocolate. Well, if you lived next door to the Savoy Ballroom, you'd hustle. It was a magnet, a force of nature that is difficult to describe to young people today who hear music in stadiums or through headphones. There we were in Harlem, and every weekend, there was a constant flow of folks coming up there with big rolls of cash they were down to flash. Everyone came through the Savoy—from Frank Sinatra and Louis Armstrong to Ella Fitzgerald and Lena Horne. We opened doors for every cab that rolled up from downtown, and they would hand us money like it was nothing. But our real thing was performing right there out in front of the Savoy. We were the pregame show, the performance before the performance.

My crew and I would go down to LC's ice cream factory down by the Harlem River, and we'd walk away with a stack of empty canisters. Then down by the Savoy, those ice cream buckets became drums, congas, timbales, or any kind of percussion you could imagine. Give us half a dozen ice cream canisters, and we could hold a beat. Then a couple of the fellas in my crew would keep drums going while the rest of us would sing harmonies. This wasn't any effort to do any kind of Harlem or even Motown sound. We took it to the "way-back machine" and sang the old standards that fit the tastes of the swells striding in from their cabs and limousines. Think about songs like "My Bonnie Lies Over the Ocean" or "Swanee River." The guys would do a little soft-shoe dance to our ice cream bucket drumbeat, and then I was in charge of hustling around asking for gratuities for our top-notch performance. It was really something special. Sometimes people would say that we were the real show, and then they would just go into the Savoy for drinks.

One individual who used to come through the Savoy on a regular basis was Fred Astaire, the dancer and movie star. Astaire would always stop to watch us, tapping his foot to the beat. Then he'd never fail to flip us a silver dollar. Please remember that this was a time when a silver dollar was like all the money in the world to us kids. As he walked away, he'd say,

"You kids always give a good show for the money." Fred Astaire didn't know it, but he gave me something that has stayed with me throughout my life. Whether I was running track, playing football, or speaking to young kids, I was going to make sure that I gave people a show. Astaire taught us that you had better give a damn about the value of flair.

But that wasn't all I learned at the Savoy. No, the education was much deeper than that. Here I was in Harlem, and the majority of people coming into our uptown paradise were white people coming from downtown. I also saw how even when our African American royalty, "Satchmo," Ella, "Lady Day," would be performing, they would always have to go in through the back door. This spoke to me in a very special way. Growing up in Harlem, I didn't know I was "black." I was a human being: Johnny Carlos, son of Earl Carlos. That's who I was. But going down to the Savoy I saw who was serving up the good times and who was being served. I saw who ate well and who provided the entertainment. It made my mind work overtime, thinking about issues that young people shouldn't have to ponder. Seeing the great black performers every week made my buttons burst with pride; at the same time I wondered why they had to sing for their supper.

The issues mattered to me because I was starting to realize in these preteen years that I also had a set of skills people would pay to watch.

Athletics

The great challenge is to put it into words. I always knew I was different just because of the way I could move, the way my body felt the breeze whip by when I would pump my legs. From the time I first laced up sneakers, I just felt this sense of being quicker and stronger than the next person. It was just a fact of life. I first figured it out in the neighborhood: not on the track, but in the dust and on street corners. I figured it out in circumstances that weren't a game. My older brothers didn't like to fight. They were four years, five years older than me, and they didn't want to, as we said, "throw hands." Unfortunately, the more they didn't want to fight, the more other people wanted to fight them. I would have to go out and take on their bullies. It was like my family chore. I would have to go out and keep those big kids off my brothers. It's true that I was smaller, but my hands and my feet both had a life of their own. After I landed a couple of jabs, or after some big corner boys realized they couldn't lay a hand on me because of my speed, they would come to the correct conclusion that the Carlos boys weren't worth the trouble.

People who saw me fight kept trying to get me involved with sports. Being good at sports meant status, it meant style, and it meant you were noticed. For me this was particularly attractive because I was the kid wearing the dunce cap in the corner at school. That's not just an expression. My teacher literally made me wear a dunce cap in the corner. Back then, the word "dyslexia" wasn't even in the dictionary, but dyslexia was my affliction, and school was an exercise in humiliation. Sports saved me from being an outcast. Ask anyone who's been called a "dumb jock," and as nasty a phrase as that is, it's certainly preferable to just being called "dumb."

When I started playing sports, the last thought on my mind was taking part in track and field. Running is what you did to get away from bullies or the police. Running is what you did to train for other sports. It never crossed my mind that track and field would be my calling. I played basketball and could certainly hang on the courts. But so much time was spent wasted on arguing over who fouled whom and talking trash that it bored more than inspired me. I was the guy who wouldn't high-five any teammates or say a word except to yell at people, "Just play the damn game!" After a while, I was turned off.

I wanted a sport where chatter wasn't a part of the equation and maybe that's why my first love was swimming. I was intrigued with absolutely anything that had to do with water. At that time, it just seemed like every single time I turned on the radio, I heard about another person swimming the English Channel. First of all, I wanted to know what in the world was the English Channel, why in the world he was trying to swim it, and what would he possibly get in return for doing it? My father explained to me that the English Channel was a substantial body of water, and he was probably swimming that great distance to establish a record, or he's doing it for self-satisfaction, or perhaps for just a measure of fame. That just sparked more questions. "Well if he's swimming it, how does he swim? Does he swim with a knife in his mouth? How does he fight the sharks off? What happens when he needs to go to the bathroom?"

My curiosity took over, and I would constantly be asking my father questions about the art of swimming. This was like asking a bald man about his favorite shampoos. My father was not a swimmer himself. He used to always tease me and say he swam like a rock: straight to the bottom. But he was a good man, and even though he didn't know a blip about swimming, he took time off work to go to the public library and research exactly how a person would begin to go about the task of swimming the English Channel—just so he could answer my question. Remember this is before the Internet. Research wasn't something a shoemaker and sharecropper's son did easily. But he did it, and piece by piece, he explained to me exactly how a person would go about swimming the English Channel. "Well that's what I want to do," I said. "I want to swim the English Channel."

Olympics

Of course I listened to every sport on the radio, but nothing captured my mind, heart, and spirit quite like the Olympic Games. When I first learned about the existence of the Olympics, my reaction was different than anything I had ever felt when listening to baseball or basketball or football or any of the other sports that I'd seen people play in the neighborhood. The sheer variety of sports, the idea of the finest athletes from around the globe gathering and representing their countries: it was different, and the fact that it was every four years just made it feel like an extra kind of special.

I asked my father about it, and he told me, "John, this is where all the nations in the world put their problems aside and focus on athletic competition." He explained the medal system—gold, silver, and bronze—and said to me, "You would have to be one of the top three in order to win any medal, and those who make it to that platform are the ones who can really, honestly, and truly be classified as one of the greatest." That just enhanced my desire to make it as a swimmer, and now I could add to my dream that not only was I going to swim the English Channel, not only was I going to go to the Olympics, but based on the history my father had laid out for me, I was going to be the first black to represent America in the water. I was twelve years old, and I just knew that this was what I needed to do: I wanted to make the Olympic team and win a medal. I would do whatever it took to make it happen.

I just loved being in that pool and my great aspiration was to go to the Olympics as a swimmer. I liked swimming freestyle and with little training I won a citywide 200-meter freestyle championship.

Swim club coaches and officials took me aside and told me that if I took my raw skills, and put in a lot of grueling, serious work, they could see me taking it all the way to the Olympics. Now I might not have liked talking trash on the court or in the pool, but on the corners, I ran my mouth and talked it up all the time. I would say, "Mark it down, Johnny Carlos is going to go to the Olympics as a swimmer!"

I talked about it every day, and it got the point where my daddy, after talking around it for some time, decided to have our "come to Jesus" talk. It was in his shoe shop. He had heard me running my mouth, and so he decided he had to do something that I know was incredibly difficult for such a good man: he intervened on my dream. Remember, Earl Carlos was an older man who had made the journey from the cotton fields to a shop near the Cotton Club. He took me aside, his eyes heavy with what he felt like he had to say. "Johnny, I don't want to see those hopes get up too high," he said. He said it as gently as he could, but he made it clear to me that I was going down a path where there would be more barriers than opportunity. To make it as an Olympic swimmer, you needed private coaches, private pools, and pay-to-play swim clubs. He just wanted me to see the hard facts in front of my face. But dreams die hard. I loved swimming so much, so I kept raising arguments.

Finally this sixty-two-year-old man took his twelve-year-old son by the shoulders and said to me, "John, you're not going to be able to go to the Olympics for swimming. It's not about the fact that you're the best. I know you're the best. But you need to listen to me, and I will say it again: there is nowhere you can train. And you have to train to go to the Olympics. So where would you train?"

You never think about that as a kid. You just think you're Superman. You just do it. And he repeated the question: "No, son, where would you train?" And he pointed out that I couldn't train in the Harlem River because two or three kids every summer would drown trying to swim in the Harlem River. "You can't go to the public pool because there's no room to train because everybody's in there trying to cool off," he said. Then he read my mind. "And you can't go to a private club," he said.

"Why not Daddy?" I asked. "Is it because you can't afford to pay for me to join a club? You know I work at the Savoy and I work in the shop. We can do it!" He shook his head and said, "No, Johnny, it's not that." I started to get angry. "Well what is it?" I demanded. And he said, "The color of your skin."

"What do you mean the color of my skin?" I asked. He said, "Well this is why they haven't had any black swimmers up until this point to represent America, because they don't allow the blacks to join the private clubs. And you have to be involved in a club that's connected to the Olympic people in order to train." He explained that they train three times a day in the finest pools with the best coaches, and that just wasn't a place where I'd be welcome—because of the color of my skin.

Now keep in mind, and I say this with humility, no one ever had to tell me that black was beautiful. I grew up in Harlem and let's just say that even at the tender age of twelve, I had these beauties at the Savoy calling me tall, dark, and handsome. My ego needed its own zip code. And now here I was hearing that because of the way I looked, I'd be on the outside looking in. It didn't make sense. It was like hearing that the sky was green.

All the worse, the person opening my eyes to this piece of knowledge was the proudest, strongest man I knew. Unless Earl Carlos was fixing shoes, he was never on his knees. Daddy tried to break the tension by cracking some jokes, saying he could train me if I wanted to come in last. I remember smiling, but it was a gesture for him and not for me. I was dejected and depressed. For the first time in my life, racism had bitten me and left a mark. For the first time, I felt like something less than others. The dream to swim had been snatched away.

Without question, there were public pools in Harlem. But you had to take only one look at these pools and see that they weren't fit for serious swimming. There was a pool in my neighborhood called Colonial Pool where all the black kids and parents would go during the summer to cool off and splash around. It was only open in the summer and you would have kids jumping in with their jeans on or wearing sneakers. I knew that the Colonial Pool wasn't an option. A short train ride away was a well-tended public pool with empty lanes that served a white neighborhood. I asked my Daddy if we could go there every week to practice. I was getting desperate and honestly, I knew what he was going to say, but I had to hear him say it. "Well, Johnny, let's talk that out," he said. "You've crashed that pool before. What happened when you and your friends jumped in the water?" I didn't have to say the answer because Earl Carlos knew. When we jumped in the water, the parents would get up and call their kids out, like something was going to roll off us and roll onto them. It was like the way people would run if there was a dead animal or something worse floating in the water. Before, I thought it was a neighborhood thing, that they didn't want outsiders in their pool. At that moment I realized that it wouldn't have mattered if I lived next door to the pool. The problem was skin-deep.

My dad saw the look on my face, processing a whole series of emotions. He was a blunt man and made no apologies for that. He said to me, "This is the exact reason why you need to get it through your head that you will never be an Olympic swimmer. Whether it's a public pool or private pool, if you can't even get in the water, then you better believe that this is done before it even starts." Then he looked at me with a challenging look, because he knew his son like he knew himself. "Swimming is out," he said. "So what are you going to do? What are you prepared to do about it? Will this stop you from making it to the Olympics?"

My face, which was all twisted with sadness, became more of a serious scowl. "No, Daddy, I ain't letting that stop me," I said. "I'm going to have to do something else." It was on to the next sport, and it was a very logical choice, given some of my "extracurricular" activities. This time I was going to make it in boxing. In short order, I put swimming out of my mind and joined the Golden Gloves. I was already throwing hands on the corners, protecting my brothers, and with the gloves on, it was just the same game with less bruising on my knuckles. In the ring, I could put a man to sleep with either hand, and people started whispering in my ear that this would in fact be my ticket to the Olympic Games.

There was one problem with this plan, and that was the one opponent I had no hope of defeating: Mama. If my Daddy pulled me out of the pool, Mama yanked those gloves right off my twelve-year-old hands. Mama stepped in and said that I was her baby boy and she would not sit by and see me get hurt or my sweet face marked up. She wasn't emotional about it. Remember, Mama was a nurse working the night shift. That means she saw what's called "blunt force trauma" on a daily basis. She knew even back then that there was a lot more to boxing than ending up with a busted lip or a bloody nose. Back then in the gym, they called it getting "punchy." She knew it as a concussion. Today we know so much more about how getting those concussions at a young age ruins your life when you get older.

Mama normally had trouble making me do anything, but even when you're a born-troublemaking-breech-birth baby like me, I couldn't defy her. When mom looks you in the eye and makes you promise to stop doing something, you do it. She looked at me across our kitchen table, her hands folded nervously in her lap, and made me say it: "I promise you that I will quit boxing." I looked at my hands and I knew I could put a man down for the count with either hand. It was a gift, but it was a gift I had to let go.

I gritted my teeth and did it for her. Now that I'm on the older side of life, with my mind sharp as it is, I'm forever grateful to her.

Now we were all clear that it wasn't going to be boxing, and I still dreamed of the Olympics, but wasn't sure what would be next on the list. I still never imagined it would be track and field. We would, when there was nothing to do, have races around the projects, around the ditches and through the gutters, and I would leave my crew in the dust. But to me, running meant three things. It was what you did to train for other sports, it was what you did to deliver messages as fast as possible through the projects for the grown-ups—our version of the Internet—and it was what you did to escape the police. That last reason was at the heart of my extracurricular activities, and it's what eventually made people notice my running to the point where I finally found my calling.

Robin Hood

I used to love the movie *Robin Hood* with Errol Flynn. I loved seeing the adventures of the man who robbed from the rich to give to the poor. I led a crew of young men who committed ourselves to doing the same thing, and the streets of Harlem were our Sherwood Forest. After all, I didn't have the option to swim and I wasn't allowed to box. I needed some extracurricular activity and I had the energy to do something.

It was always a simple plan. I would lead my crew under cover of night and break into the freight trains that would be parked right across from us under the 155th Street Bridge. These trains were barely guarded and were easy pickings. Each of us would pick up 25-pound boxes of food, make our way back across the bridge, and feed people in the community. I would be running with two boxes—that's 50 pounds on my shoulders—coming across that bridge. Even with that weight, I would be able to outrun the night watchmen and the police.

This on its own gave me a reputation in the community. People would watch from their windows and say, "That boy Johnny Carlos can outrun the guards and the police with 50 pounds on his shoulders!" As time went on, this unique exercise made me stronger and stronger, from my shoulders down to my thighs. I didn't realize that this "exercise" in giving back to the people was also giving me a level of physical training that, coupled with natural speed, would put me on a world stage.

I'm well aware that all this might sound strange: breaking into freight trains and carrying 50 pounds on my shoulders and then giving all the food to the poorest people in Harlem. Hell, it sounds strange to me now, but at the time it made a whole lot of sense. A lot of the men in Harlem at this particular time were missing in action. There were a lot of fathers that were MIA from their families. There were a lot of mothers trying to raise kids on their own. There were a lot of men being swallowed up by the drugs, the heroin that we called "King Kong," the lack of jobs, or the prisons. It was difficult or even damn near impossible for a single mother to raise a family if she had two or three kids. When a parent was missing in action, that meant a lot of kids didn't have anything in their iceboxes or cupboards. We are talking about more than empty bellies. We are talking about food deprivation, just walking distance from the Cotton Club.

I understood how lucky I was—in my own house, with two parents who worked day and night and made a stable living. That's not to mention two brothers and a sister doing the same. We had a five-income household! On a regular basis, I would bring a lot of my buddies home to eat lunch, and then they'd come back uninvited, like stray puppy dogs, for dinner. I remember Mama saying, "Johnny, I hate to break it to you, but we can't feed everybody. This is a home, not a cafeteria!" I knew she was right, but at the same time, I thought what I was doing was even more right. But I didn't have control over my Mama's kitchen. My friends—and the friends of my friends, and their friends—needed to eat as well. I needed another way to get them food because Mama was going to put a padlock on the icebox if I wasn't careful. I needed another plan. I knew they had the freight trains over there in the yards outside of the old Yankee Stadium. Three of my partners and I began to go on expeditions. These were the three guys in my crew whom I was absolutely tightest with and I knew wouldn't breathe a word of this to anybody. I told them, "Man, we're going to go over to those freight trains and see what those guys have inside that we can circulate into the community." My boys asked if we were going to get paid. I said, "Fellas. This isn't about us. This is about Robin Hood. We are hitting those trains and putting it right onto the streets of Harlem." On our first trip over, our stomachs were a mess of nerves. We didn't know what was on those trains. We didn't know if a watchman or some drifter with a blade might be about, but most of all none of us wanted to end up in juvie. We stepped softly on the trains, around some sleeping security guard, and made it into the storage car. It was filled top to bottom with frozen foods: every vegetable from spinach to succotash. The next car was filled with baby clothes. It was everything we needed in Harlem and didn't have—and it was right across the bridge! What would Robin Hood do?

Standing there in that train car, my crew looked at me, and we all had the same question: "Were we actually going to go through with this?" At that moment I had my doubts. My father was a very serious-minded man, a very strong American, a veteran, and someone who hated racism but loved his country and thought he went through hell in the First World War to make this place better for black folks. My mother had that same character, working the night shift—and the two of them being as charitable and honest a pair of parents as anyone could ever hope to have in their lives. They brought up the Carlos children to walk the straight and narrow, to respect the law of the land, and they pounded this into our heads at every opportunity.

I was as frozen as that succotash standing in that car, hearing their voices in my head. But I heard different voices swirling around at the same time. I didn't want to go against anything my father and mother taught us to believe in, but I couldn't deny that those voices felt more connected to my heart and soul. These voices spoke to me of the fact that all across the South people were breaking a law called Jim Crow. Dr. Martin Luther King Jr. was a God in my mother's eyes and wasn't he breaking the law? And that's when it came into my mind that there are always two laws that need to be weighed: man's law and God's law, and God put food everywhere on the planet before man stepped in. God made this earth so no child would ever have to go to sleep with a rumble in their tummy or not have clothes. That was the law I was ready to follow and to die for.

I looked at my buddies and told them, "Alright, fellas, load up and get those boxes on your shoulders and let's run." We then went around Harlem handing out food and clothes like *Robin Hood and His Merry Men* in Technicolor. We had a reputation for doing the right thing and being able to lose ourselves in the shadows. But often times, we escaped just by the skin of our teeth. Often we had to think and plan ahead. One night, we navigated across the 155th Street Bridge. There was a man in charge of opening up the bridge when the ferryboats would ride through. All night, he would sit in this little box and run the bridge. For security purposes, he had a radio to call the police if he saw anything out of sorts. But, unless the police told him otherwise, he was just content to sit in his box, read the paper, and put up his feet. I went to him and said, "My crew has been hitting these trains and giving the goods out to the people. The police have been chasing us, and one of these days, they are going to wise up and ask you to open this bridge to trap us on the other side."

"Yeah, I see you guys running all the time," he said. "Should be just a matter of time before they ask me to hem you up."

"How much money do they pay you to sit in this box?" I asked him. "They don't pay me nearly enough," he replied. So I said, "Well, what if every time we cross with our boxes, we dropped you something off, a care package of whatever we find on these trains. How does that sound to you?" He smiled like the sly, past-his-prime hustler he was and said, "Now this is a conversation I'm ready to have." But I shook my head and said, "Not so fast, friend. We need you to do more than just look the other way. We need you to agree to hem us in, but really give us five minutes to run across the bridge before you raise it and trap us on the other side. Just five minutes. That's all I ask." He laughed and shot back, "I can't give you five before I have to open it. That would tip off the police that we'd been talking and I'd lose my job that very night. No deal."

"Well what *can* you do?" I asked. "You're not going to like it, but I can give you three extra minutes," he replied. "I can say that it takes three minutes to get the gear in order and lift the bridge. But I don't see how you can run across that bridge with those boxes and make it across the river." Three minutes was nothing easy, but I knew I had that speed so I said, "Don't worry. We can do it." It was a done deal. We were ready. We now had a system to escape the police, and we were able to get those crates on our shoulders, hit that third gear and make it across that bridge in three minutes, from the Bronx back to Harlem.

A lot of people in the neighborhood started to whisper about me as we ran through the streets, giving out food and clothes. When the whispers got back to me, I was surprised that the whispers were less for the merchandise than for the speed I showed the audience watching from the tenement windows. At this particular time in New York's history, the police were mostly Irish and they had these beer bellies. Many people thought that this made them slow, but those beer bellies fooled many a cocky street soldier. These police could run like whippets, their bellies jiggling up and down over their belts. They would chase us down like they were Jesse Owens. The slower runners in my crew would be grabbed on the run by their back collars and thrown roughly against the nearest wall. Whenever this would happen, a crowd would develop like they would every time a white cop had a young brother against the wall. I would always circle back and stand in the crowd, and I'd be among everyone else, instigating. I'd be saying, "What did they do? Why y'all bothering them? Leave them alone! What's going on here? This is Harlem, not Mississippi!" My boys would look around and see me there, and they would be up against the wall, and they'd be fighting a smile because they knew I made it free. They would also smile because they knew that sometimes this would cause enough tension that the police would just cuff their ears and let them walk. At the time, I never looked at it from the sense of me having any kind of particular talent as a runner. I was just a kid doing what kids do, the difference being that I just happened to be uncatchable while I was doing it.

While I was in the process of developing this public reputation as Robin Hood on skates, I had to lead a double life at home. My brothers and my sister couldn't know about it. My Mom couldn't know about it, and my Dad in particular couldn't know about it. If he ever found out that I was robbing trains, I wouldn't have been able to sit down for a week. I already knew that his belt was at the ready. Back then it was easy to play hooky. Too easy. A lot of kids would walk through the front door of school and just walk right out the back. I did get caught playing hooky one day by my mom, and when she told Earl Carlos, there was hell to pay. My father was very fond of saying that he was "captain of the ship." When I played hooky, it was like I was engaging in mutiny. He then did what he would do—he "fired me up" on my behind with his leather belt.

But even though the risk of robbing trains and playing Robin Hood was great, it felt right. It felt right to give people groceries and then when they reached for their sparest of spare change, explain that this wasn't anything we were doing for any kind of monetary gain for ourselves. I told them this was not for us to sell. We said, "Nobody is trying to get big pockets from raiding the trains." We are going to give this to the people who didn't have any food. In today's times, no one would have believed us and honestly, if one of the schoolkids I mentor told me they weren't doing it for monetary gain, I would look at them more than a little cross-eyed. But these were the times. People believed me because community, civil rights, and challenging authority were all in the air.

But even if I could cross the authority of the police, the truant officers, and the night watchmen at the train, the one authority I knew I had to step gingerly around was that of Earl Carlos. This eventually caught up with me when, at the age of fifteen, I took a turn away from giving away goods from the train to selling marijuana cigarettes.

Although I didn't smoke it, it was just another hustle to fill my pockets after school. I would go down with my crew to the famous dance club the Palladium, all the way downtown, and we'd sell joints, a dollar each. By the time we made it back to the house, our pockets were so fat, it looked like we were walking with saddle bags. But one day, my Mama was cleaning out my closet and she found some serious contraband: it was a plastic bag of rolled up marijuana cigarettes. On this one evening in particular, my buddy Cliff and I came back to the Carlos family apartment at three in the morning, and thought we would be fine because at that time, my mother would be on the night shift at the hospital and my father would be out like a light. His goal on most weeknights was just to make it until the eight o'clock news. If you're going to open a shop at seven in the morning, you'd better be asleep well before three.

But wouldn't you know, as we tiptoed through the front door, there was Earl Vanderbilt Carlos waiting for us, pacing like he was going to wear a path in the carpet.

First he said, "Cliff, sit down. Johnny, get into your room." I walked into my room and there it was on my bed: every last bit of contraband I owned had been laid out from my closet. It was a lot of marijuana, but to my eyes, it looked a little light. I looked over my shoulder and my father was standing there with steam coming out of his ears. Maybe it's because it was 3 a.m., and my mouth was moving faster than my brain, but I turned around and I said, "Where's the rest of my supply?" Bad move. Without a word, the belt came out and he fired me up good.

Then came the discussion, although it wasn't much of a discussion. It was me sitting and hearing those quiet words of disappointment that to my memory stung more sharply than any belt. My daddy, I found out at that moment, knew that we had been stealing from the yards, and boosting from the department stores, and giving away goods in the streets of Harlem. He saw that I had crates of merchandise in the pipeline of my fantasy of being an Uptown Robin Hood.

But he also knew that drugs were an entirely different story and that I had taken the hustle to a place that he could not abide. I remember this as clearly as if I had it on a home movie. He said,

I don't know how you got all these boxes out. I don't know how you are doing all this. And I'm not going to judge too hard because I did some sideways moves myself at your age. But when you bring dope into my house, you've crossed the line. What you're doing here will bring the weight of the law onto this family. The police will kick down this door, put us out of our home, and put a black mark on every member of this family. They could send your mother to jail, your brothers to jail, your sister to jail, and me too. I didn't get shot at in Europe in that damn war just to see my family end up in that state. You don't even have sense enough to realize what jeopardy you putting your family in.

I felt terrible and agreed with his every point. I quietly apologized up and down in a way that he knew I meant it. Then he said, "I'm glad that my baby boy has grown up to be a man. Glad and surprised. I promise I will never ever hit you with the belt again."

I gave him all my contraband and accepted that he would flush it right down the toilet. But that's not where this story ends. Twenty years later, my father passed away after a rich, long life. As I stood by the gravesite, my uncle came up and said, "Remember that problem with your daddy with the marijuana about twenty years back?"

I'd forgotten about it, but I laughed sadly and said, "Yeah, I remember." Then my uncle said, "Well I guess I can tell you now because your Daddy is gone, but he only pretended to flush all that weed. He and I have been smoking that very supply for the last twenty years. Just a little taste every week." I thought that was the funniest thing I'd ever heard in my entire life because I thought my father didn't smoke anything but a cigar or a pipe. But he had about eight pounds of the stuff, and wasn't nobody smoking it but him and my uncle.

Malcolm Little

The experience of stealing groceries and goods and giving the people something for nothing was positive. Just doing this kind of so-called work opened up my mind and got me to notice what was going on around me. I couldn't turn my back when I saw evidence of discrimination in the community. I captured it in my mind every time I saw anyone in my neighborhood mistreated by the police. I also made a point to remember the way people in Harlem were mistreated by the fire department as well. Imagine if you had smoke coming out of your kitchen window or you left some beans on the stove. The fire department would burst in as a matter of course, and break down the doors, chop up the furniture and destroy everything you had. I just knew they didn't do this on Fifth Avenue or it would have made the papers. But in Harlem, anytime you called the police or the fire department, you did it with the stone-cold knowledge that you could be inviting in forces beyond your control. They didn't have any people of color in the fire department at that time so fear replaced reason. They feared what could be lurking behind every door or dark corner in Harlem more than they feared the fire. When people took the chance and called the police, it could result in an even worse outcome. Imagine being a woman suffering a home break-in or even domestic abuse and being scared to call the police out of fear of those who were supposed to serve and protect.

When I started seeing these things more thoughts started to mushroom in my brain. I understood that something wasn't quite right with the world and it went beyond little Johnny Carlos not having a place to practice his swimming, and it was a problem that couldn't be solved with a couple of cartons of frozen succotash.

I want to be clear. It's not like I was the only one who saw there was a problem. On every street corner, it seemed, you had someone preaching about the evils of the world. This made me less like a misfit than I might have otherwise been. All around you in Harlem were people ready to speak out against the ills of the world, and you took as a starting point that yes, there were ills that stretched above and beyond people's personal responsibility. On the soapboxes, there were without question more than a few charlatans, but there were also magnetic speakers with something to say. One of them even ended up on a postage stamp. It was just impossible to grow up in the late 1950s and early 1960s in Harlem, USA, without feeling the presence of the man who came into this world as Malcolm Little and who died as Malik El-Shabazz. We of course knew him as Malcolm X.

Growing up in Harlem at this time, it was hard to not have memories—vivid memories—of Malcolm X. When I was fourteen, I watched as Malcolm arrived at 116th Street, for the ceremonial opening of a new mosque for the Nation of Islam. I wanted to be there because I had seen him speak on the corners and heard snippets of him debating and just decimating people on the radio. I had heard him discussed more than a few times in barbershops and the schoolyard. It was Malcolm this and Malcolm that and I wanted to see it and hear it for myself, on his home turf and in his mosque.

Arriving at 116th Street, I was seated in a packed house at the mosque. Most of the people there for the opening gave no indication that they were members of the Nation of Islam. I was one of many there to hear what this great man had to say and honestly, in my memory of that day, I remember being blown away. Malcolm didn't speak like Dr. King or Representative Adam Clayton Powell or any of the church-trained speakers I'd ever seen. It was like he was blowing out my eardrums without raising his voice. He didn't perform any kind of theatrics with either his pitch or his tone. There was no showmanship in the man. His power, and the response of the audience, grew out of the fact that he was articulating ideas we were thinking about all the time but didn't really have a language or vocabulary to express. For me, it was like he grabbed onto my frustrations and turned them into logic.

On that day, standing as straight as a sentry and with the confidence of a CEO, Malcolm spoke about trying to build character and confidence among our people. He said that he looked out onto Harlem and saw no self-esteem or pride in who we were as people. Malcolm wasn't speaking to the best angels of our nature. He was speaking to the distance we had to travel if we were going to be seen and respected as human beings, not animals, servants, or slaves. At that time, even as a young fourteen-year-old, it felt like we were being confronted with every possible challenge—unemployment, drugs, broken families—challenges that would bury the best of us. But we lacked the skills: the character, the faith, the community, to handle these terribly difficult situations. Malcolm knew how to speak to that in a very special, focused kind of way. He would break you down and make you feel a sense of hope that we could find our way back. No one who has merely seen *Malcolm X* or seen Malcolm in documentaries can understand the charisma this man had. That first time hearing Malcolm speak just touched me and moved me so strongly that I felt like an addict hooked on the first shot, that first message.

It drew me back and I returned to the mosque every time I caught word that he would be there to speak. It came to the point that I was there so much that I learned his schedule and I would wait around for when Malcolm was done and, if he was walking the streets, I would follow him from one location to another like a scampering puppy dog. He was such a fast walker, and he would be hustling to get to his next location. I hadn't had my growth spurt yet so I would have to do a little jog just to keep up alongside him. It was actually good exercise for me. Looking back, it must have been the most unique workout regimen for an Olympic hopeful: stealing boxes off trains and trailing after Malcolm X. What made it serious work was that Malcolm never, ever slowed down for me, but when I could keep up, he gave me the opportunity to walk with him and fire questions at him. I guess it amused him—me running alongside him—but when I asked him my questions, he took me as seriously as a heart attack. I had two big questions that I still remember asking him: "Why do you believe what you believe?" I asked, "And why aren't there more individuals out there doing what you are doing?"

He always said that he believed that people out there were aware of the same injustices that he was aware of. He said that the success of the Nation of Islam and the crowds he was commanding were proof of that fact. But the people who were coming to hear him speak didn't stand with him in bigger numbers because we were so fragmented as a people. He was remarkably without ego. He never said that maybe people came out to hear him speak because they wanted to hear him speak!

We became more or less accustomed to one another and he knew after he got through speaking that if I was there, I would be running alongside his long-legged steps. I did this both when he was with the Nation of Islam and after he grew out his beard and left that particular organization. I believed in the man. For the next five years, as I became bigger, stronger, and better known in the community, I still always made it down to hear him speak. He definitely got a kick out of the fact that the little boy who used to run alongside him was getting known as a teenage sprinter.

But I wasn't there on February 21, 1965, the day Malcolm was assassinated. This sticks in my throat to this day. On the day Malcolm was violently taken from us while speaking onstage at the Audubon Ballroom, I was outside the city. I was trying to get my driver's license and a friend had taken me to the country so I could practice on some lonely roads. On our way back into the five boroughs, the music was interrupted by the horrible news that Malcolm had been shot. Immediately my partner and I changed the route we were taking and went straight to the Audubon. There we learned what hospital he'd been taken to and we jumped up there like a flash.

By the time we made it to the hospital, everyone was milling around outside—shouting, angry, crying, huddled against the wall—and the word quickly traveled to us that Malcolm was dead. He'd been gunned down. It probably took fifteen or twenty years before a day went by that I didn't think about it. Some days I wondered if I'd ever be able to stop thinking about it.

The memory of Malcolm's assassination still has some effect on me because I felt like if I was in that ballroom that night, maybe I would have seen something or noticed something and maybe he wouldn't have been shot. I know that doesn't sound too logical and I can't explain it in a way that makes sense. It just took a lot out of me for a long time because I had a feeling that in some way, shape, or form, I would have been able to do something to intervene. I was just in love with the man. Maybe it was because he made time for me on the streets. Maybe it was because he made me raise my head up high. But it definitely always seemed like he was two steps ahead of the rest of us. He saw the protests against Jim Crow in the South and demanded to know whether such a thing would work in the North. He challenged the legitimacy and seriousness of either of the two dominant political parties to take the realities of racism seriously.

He went to Mecca and achieved the awesome realization that white folks, Arabs, Indians, Puerto Ricans had it inside them to treat him like a brother and fully formed human being. It was anybody and everybody over there at Mecca. He knew that we could build a movement, unite as a people, and make it work by any means necessary. He knew that it wouldn't be based on skin color but as he said, "oppressor versus oppressed." That's what made him so dangerous to so many.

Two

■　　■　　■　　■

Street Level Protest:
"You Have Forty-Eight Hours . . ."

Malcolm gave me the verbal justification and political confidence to do what I always felt in my gut: to act. People talked about the South and civil rights in those days, but Malcolm always said that we had to get our struggle on point up in the North, where there was no Jim Crow but a whole hell of a lot of problems. In high school I had several moments where I went out of my way to put myself in a position to engage in street-level protest. I'll never forget when my crew and I were sitting in the high school cafeteria at our own table and everyone was talking about how god-awful the nasty slop they called "food" was that they served us. We were talking about how they put the same damn thing on our plates every day: chicken, which we all knew was the food of poor people.

When I say the food of poor people, I'm not knocking it. It's a long-running joke or stereotype that black folks eat chicken wings and love fried chicken. It's more than just a stereotype, though, because our people have always eaten chicken, going back to the plantations. It's not just black folk. Any kind of people who don't have a powerful income can buy a chicken and cook it up at least fifty different ways. We used to eat a lot of chicken at the Carlos household and my Mama could make that chicken dance. But at school it was different. Whether it was broiled chicken or roast chicken or baked chicken or fried chicken, chicken soup or chicken salad, the food wasn't fresh or clean. Back then, we didn't know salmonella from smoked salmon, but we knew enough to know that there shouldn't be feathers in our food. We weren't Rockefellers, but we knew that every day the school was sending us a message that we were lower than dirt, symbolized by these nasty chickens.

My crew was getting plenty steamed about it saying, "Yeah, man, when we bite into the chicken, we got feathers all up in our mouth." They were angry but they also seemed content to just complain. I said, "Yeah, this is a bad thing going on here, but this is also a time when we can do something about it. We can stop this right away." I said that we most likely couldn't make them give us a whole new menu every day, but we could damn sure make them stop feeding us undercooked chicken with the feathers in it.

The next day I put it in my plans to discuss the matter with the school principal. I walked into his office first thing in the morning and I said, "Sir, I would like to speak with you about the conditions of our food in the cafeteria." He barely looked up from his desk and told me just to get the heck out of his office. I spoke sharply back, "What do you mean, get out of your office? I'm a student and I have a right to be here. I have a right to speak my mind and state that we need a better quality of food." He sighed and looked up from his desk and spoke to me in a slow, simple voice as if I were five years old. He explained, in that slow voice, that the school received the chicken parts in bulk every day and it was impossible to expect the cafeteria workers to properly care for our food. I told him, "My mother does it every day and if my Momma can do it, y'all can do it." Then he gave me a look like I was lower than low and told me to get out. He lowered his eyes to get back to whatever he was doing, but I didn't move. Then he raised his voice to me to get to stepping, but I just stood there, ramrod straight like Malcolm and stared into his eyes. That's when he pulled back from his desk, stood up tall, and pushed me out of his office. Yes, he physically pushed me out of his office, which back then was something school officials could do without worrying about being sued. He slammed the door and I stumbled, almost losing my balance. Then I steeled and collected myself, took a deep breath, and walked back into his office and said, "Man, you have forty-eight hours to take care of it."

When you call the principal, "man," you get their attention. But what made him really perk up was the fact that I had put him on notice. When you look in someone's eyes and say, "You have forty-eight hours to take care of it," the first thing that comes into their mind is that they're being threatened in some way and sure enough, the principal exploded in a rage and said, "Are you threatening me? Is that what you just did?!" I didn't ever want to get caught in a situation of having a principal say I threatened him. There was no win in that for fifteen-year-old Johnny Carlos. But I did say, "No, that's not a threat, but a money-back guarantee. If you don't handle it, I will."

Now I had forty-eight hours to figure out exactly how I was going to make good on my big words. We quickly rounded up the crew and worked out a plan. Of course the forty-eight hours came and went and the principal didn't do a damn thing to clean up our undercooked, feathered food.

It was time to take action. I said to my crew, "Alright, they had their move, now we have ours." So we put the word out there that we were going on a cafeteria strike. We were going to boycott the school food like we were bus riders in Montgomery, Alabama. We told everyone not to buy cafeteria food but to brown-bag it. It would be known in the hallways as the "brown bag boycott." Almost everybody did it, but we had a couple of young folks that didn't buy into the program. I didn't know whether they didn't agree or they didn't know this was serious or they didn't get the word. But they were going around with their trays in the cafeteria and then had some unfortunate accidents, where they would swing around the corner with their trays and someone would bump and knock the tray out of their hands. This wasn't nice or pleasant, but we needed everyone 100 percent in. Even 98 percent wasn't going to cut it. Wouldn't you know, after a couple of these spills, they got the message and started brown-bagging it too.

We had this strike going on for two weeks, and the school was hurting because of it. With no one buying lunch, and all this nasty rotting food, they were feeling it. After two weeks, though, everybody was starting to get antsy about staying strong. Attention was beginning to drift and most importantly, a lot of kids didn't have the money to brown-bag it every day. So I went back to the principal with my chest puffed out and I said, "What are you going to do? Man, we've been on a strike here and you're pretending like you don't even notice but I know you want us to stop." He looked at me and said in this low voice, "I told you nothing is going to change." I held his eye and told him, "I tell you what, you said nothing is going change, I say something's going change, let's see what the public has to say." I said, "I'm going call up the *New York Times*, the *Daily News,* the Harlem press, and everyone else and see if they think they have a story here."

When I said that, it seemed like his antennae went up and he started twitching. His voice went from rough to sweet and he said, "Well John, I don't think we need to do that. Why don't you come and sit down and we can talk about this." Next thing you knew, we weren't seeing any feathers in our food. That's the first time that I saw the waters part; I saw that we could make positive change for ourselves. We didn't have to wait for some well-meaning official to do it on our behalf. We could project our will, and if we had strength and unity, we could move mountains. This was our Montgomery, our Selma, our March on Washington. I know it was just a small struggle in a small place, but just because it wasn't dramatic and historic doesn't mean it didn't change those of us at the heart of organizing such a bold response to an everyday injustice. Besides, whether it's a school cafeteria or an Olympic medal podium, you have to organize where you stand.

After the dust had cleared from this incident, I felt like I had a new slogan: "You've got forty-eight hours." I really liked the idea of putting that sentiment to someone in power and making it clear to them that I wasn't talking just to hear myself speak. I liked the idea of making it clear that there were demands that needed to be met and that I wasn't playing games. The great Frederick Douglass once said, "Power concedes nothing without a demand." That means you better come with some demands and whenever I did I always ended it by saying, "You've got forty-eight hours."

The next time I said those four fateful words, it was in the projects and it involved standing up for my beautiful, hard-working Momma. My mother, remember, was a nurse's aide down at Bellevue Hospital, working in the operating and emergency room from midnight to eight in the morning. It was an exhausting way to make a living. When she was off work, my Momma would sit upstairs in our apartment and just stare out the window. In those days, the projects were different than they are today. Back then, they had very nice courtyards and ladies would sit on the benches and talk. Compared to today, it was like an alternate universe because you don't exactly see older ladies and mothers socializing outdoors in the projects today. But back then it was just what every older lady did. My mother, however, did not. She very seldom came downstairs to sit on the benches with the other ladies. Vioris Carlos would just stare out of her window by her lonesome.

I was at an age when I both had a big mouth and needed to know everybody's business, so I asked her, "Hey, Momma! How come you don't sit downstairs? Why is it I don't see you sit with the women in the courtyard? I don't want the other moms or the other kids to think you're stuck up!" And my mother looked at me like she wanted to pop my lip and just said, "Am I stuck up? Is that what you think of your mother?" I looked down feeling both sheepish and sad because the last thing I ever wanted to do was hurt her feelings. But I was bullheaded and I persisted. I asked her, "Well, Mom, you never go downstairs and sit down with the women. Do you think you're too good for them?" And then Vioris Carlos, who saw the worst this city had to offer every night between midnight and eight in the morning, went from looking mad to looking hurt and vulnerable. She took a deep breath and said, "No Johnny, I'm not stuck up. But down there in the courtyard, the trees are infested with caterpillars. Whenever I sit down there, they fall on my neck. When I brush them away, they burst and I get these terrible rashes on my arms and my neck. I just can't stand it. The benches, the bushes . . . it's all crawling with these caterpillars and I want nothing to do with it." I knew that she was speaking the stone-cold truth. In the middle of the night, when the projects and the city were as still and as quiet as a country meadow, you could even hear the caterpillars eating the leaves on the trees. She was choking back the tears talking about this, and I was mad as hell. I was mad at myself for hurting her feelings and I was mad that my mother had to hole up in our apartment when she wasn't slaving away at the hospital.

The next day, I walked into the office of the manager of the projects with the same attitude I had when I met with the principal. I knocked on his door and before he could answer, I let myself in and said, "Sir, we need to talk, and we need to talk now." He looked up with a bit of a smirk, almost like I was his day's comic relief and he said, "What's the problem, little man?" I ignored the side comment and told the entire story about my mother and her complaints. "You, sir, are the manager of these projects. Don't you think you have a responsibility to do something about these caterpillars around here?" I asked. He told me to go wait outside in the courtyard while he made some calls and researched the matter. Then he would call me back in with an answer. I walked outside, more than satisfied that I was being listened to. I still remember that feeling of standing in the courtyard, feeling good, while the folks around me were listening to a jazzy number on the radio. I thought to myself, "Maybe these times are changing."

Five minutes later I was called back into the office and the big smile was quickly wiped off my face. This would not go well. I knew immediately something bad was going on because this old brother security guard—the police of the projects—came out from behind the door when I walked in, and stood behind me, so close his big belly was against my back. In front of me, the manager had an absolutely sick grin on his face. He said, "Thanks for coming back in. I looked into the problem and I decided that I wanted you to come back in here so I could throw you out!" Then he laughed. The security guard knew me by name if not by reputation so he said, "Come on, Johnny. We don't want no trouble." I shook him off and said, "Man, I ain't started no trouble. I'm just trying to be heard." He said, "Well you were heard and now it's over. I have to take you outside." He then gripped me by the arms and started to walk me out. But I broke out of his grip, ran back, and looked right into that mean bastard's face and said, "You've got forty-eight hours to deal with this problem or I'm going to deal with it." He got up from his chair, all confidence and condescension, and said, "Are you threatening me, boy?" The guard was playing good cop and trying to calm me down, saying, "Now, don't do that Johnny. No threats." I said back, "I'm not threatening this man, but I am giving him a forty-eight-hour guarantee—a money-back guarantee. If he don't straighten the problem out, I will!"

I waited the forty-eight hours and of course the manager didn't do a damn thing about those caterpillars. Nothing happened. I then put my personal grievance plan into action. I went around the courtyard and told all the women sitting there on the benches, "You're going to want to move to the other end of the projects, or go upstairs because something is getting ready to pop off here." Then I left the courtyard and went to a nearby gas station. The station manager was a good buddy of my father's and I told him that my daddy needed some gasoline and I didn't have a gas can. He went and got one of his old cans and filled it up with gasoline, gave it to me, and told me to just have my father stop by and pay him whenever he got the chance.

Now, I went to the courtyard in the projects, armed with my can of gasoline. A couple of people who I told to split were still hanging around the benches. I didn't know if they were people who didn't pay me any mind, or if they wanted to see what was about to go down. I told them one last time, "Y'all go somewhere else." They all looked at me with a deep wariness in their eyes and one asked, "What are you getting ready to do?" I said, "Just move on out of here. Please. It's about to get mighty hot."

Then I took the cap off the can and doused the first tree in front of me with gasoline. Then I reached for a box of long, thick wooden matches. After that first tree was soaked, I struck one of the stick matches against my zipper and threw it at the tree and watched. It was a sight: the fire just ate that tree like it was newspaper and turned it into a fireball of fried caterpillars. All the older ladies who I tried to warn off were standing on the side and started shouting, "Oh no! That Johnny Carlos! He's crazy!" They started screaming that over and over again and sure enough people started sticking their heads out of their windows, calling for help. Now, here comes the police and for the folks in the projects, seeing the police was a signal not to stand down, but to get even more excited. People started running around, taking part in the chaos, making it difficult for the police to get at me.

The police were like deer in the headlights, not sure whether they should tackle me, put out that fire, or just mind the crowd. While they paused, I figured I was in for a penny, in for a pound, and I sprayed a second tree with gas and lit that one up too. That just added to the chaos and made the atmosphere even more frazzled. Then I went and hit a third tree, and at that point they got their senses together, wrestled me to the ground, and called for the paddy wagon to pick me up and take me down to the 32nd Precinct. Even though I was a minor, I was in some serious trouble. They went through the full booking procedure and gave me a court date. When my mother brought me home, the tension in the Carlos household was at an all-time high. Nobody was happy with me, especially my mother. She did not want to hear that I had done this for her. In fact she was devastated that I even associated her with it. When it came time to go to court,

Vioris Carlos stayed away. It was on my father to stand next to me and face the judge.

The first question the judge asked my father was, "Mr. Carlos, does your son have all his faculties? Does he have any diagnosed psychological problems this court should be made aware of?" My father, who was on the other side of sixty and a First World War veteran, had to bite his lip, take a deep breath, and tell the judge, "Well your honor, to my knowledge there ain't no evidence that my son is crazier than the next child." The judge then said to my father, "Mr. Carlos, if your son has all his faculties, why would he do what he did? Why would he feel the need to burn those trees if he didn't have some sort of mental disorder?" Earl Vanderbilt Carlos looked up at that judge for a long time and finally said, "That's a good question, your honor. He's right here. I think you should put the question to him yourself." The judge then looked at me very closely. He didn't stare with hostility, but like he was a scientist examining a species he didn't understand. He said, "Son, why did you do what you did?"

When he asked, I let it all hang out. I told him the whole story about how my mother, a hard-working Bellevue nurse's aide, couldn't come downstairs and relax in our courtyard because of these nasty caterpillars. I told him that as long as I'd lived in those projects, I'd never seen anyone from the city spray the trees or take any actions against infestation. I told him that the entire situation had become unbearable and inhumane. The judge was quiet for a moment. Then he turned to the building manager, who was sitting at the table with the prosecution, and said, "Sir, surely you are aware that you get an allotment from the city every year to spray those trees to guard against infestation. Is this true that they haven't been sprayed in years? And if it is true, what is happening to the money you are receiving from the city to take care of these trees?"

The building manager turned a whiter shade of pale in front of our eyes. After a stammer and a stutter, he said, "Well I can't tell you the last time the trees were sprayed because I didn't know I'd be asked these questions and I don't have the appropriate paperwork with me at this time, your honor." The judge then stopped the trial and requested that "the appropriate paperwork" be submitted for evidence before we could continue. It was like the whole focus of the judge had shifted away from me. Now it was as if the building manager was on trial. Talk about a sign of the times!

When we continued at a later date, the judge came to discover that this joker of a building manager had been getting money to deal with infestation for fifteen years and chose to pocket it every step of the way. The judge ruled from the bench that I'd been provoked to take such drastic action, and given that I'd made every effort, according to testimony, to clear the courtyard before setting the fires, and considering that I was a juvenile, I was free to go. My father shuddered with joy next to me and gave me a squeeze that could have broken me in half.

When we got back to the projects, people slapped me on the back and called me a hero, but behind my back they were saying that I really must be crazy. People in the projects figured that normal guys would never do anything like that. But this was a time when a lot of so-called normal guys were feeling like normal just wasn't going to cut it anymore and "crazy" was the only option left on the table.

My mother and father, as grateful as they were that this had swung my way, were not trying to hear that "crazy" was the only option on the table. They were still very upset with me, but by this point, they pretty much knew the type of kid that I was. I wasn't like my sister or my brothers. If I believed in something, I was going to stay with it until the end, come hell or high water. They knew that if I had to take an ass-whupping, from them or anyone else, I was going to take that ass-whupping. I'll take it until I can't sit, but it is not going to make me back down or change my mind. But my parents weren't exactly a united front on this. My mom, remember, wouldn't even come down to court. She was raised in Cuba and was too angry, too upset with my lack of discipline, too ashamed, to see me disciplined by a judge.

My father, the sharecropper's son who fought for freedoms abroad that he didn't have at home, stood with me. No one knew better than my father that neither he nor anyone else on earth could whip me enough to make me change what I believed to be right. So, when the judge was done and I was scot-free, my father said, "Well Johnny, you turned out to be the winner in this one. It's just like the time with you and that pet chicken." I didn't know what he was talking about. As we walked down the courtroom steps, he reminded me of something that happened when I was younger.

Apparently, when I was younger, I asked my mother if I could buy a chicken and raise it. My mother looked at me like I had a screw loose and said, "No, you can't get no chicken." Well I didn't have enough money for a chicken, but I had a piggy bank, so I broke it open, took out all my savings, and went down to this place where they were selling eggs. I had enough money for a dozen farm fresh eggs and figured if I cared for them correctly, I could end up with twelve baby chicks. I went down and spoke to the local farmer and made sure I bought eggs that could conceivably hatch. Then I paid off the farmer to get his hens to hatch them for me. When I had a mess of baby chicks, I snuck all of them into the house, took them in the bathroom, and hid them in the tub. My Momma yelled down the hall, "What's all that noise?" I said, "What noise, ma? I don't hear nothing." She busted into the bathroom and saw a mess of chickadees living in her bathtub. She said, "John, you can't have these chickens." I said, "Mom, they're my chickens. I paid for them. Please let me keep them." My mother responded with that old standby, "Wait until your father gets home."

Sure enough, my father trudged home bone-tired, looked at the chicks, and he said, "Well, boy, you spent all your savings up. But you did do a good thing because you got the most out of your money. So here's what I'm going to let you do, I'm going to let you keep one chick as a pet." My mother stared some daggers through him on that one.

I took them all back to the farmer and I kept this one chick in the house. My little chickadee turned into a rooster and I treated that rooster like it was the family dog. I named him Charlie, petted his feathers, and taught him how to scratch the floor on command. Then came my elementary school's science fair and no teacher gave me a word of encouragement to enter because of my grades. But I made plans to show up with Charlie as my prize exhibit. When my momma got wind of this, she almost blew her top and didn't even want to let me out of the house. She said, "Boy, don't you dare bring that nasty rooster to your school." But I did.

At the fair, I remember all the kids showing up with these elaborate projects, charts, and diagrams hoping for that blue ribbon. As for me, I just brought Charlie. When the judges saw Charlie's act, when they saw him peck, count, and do everything but play fetch, I won the blue ribbon easily. They'd never seen a rooster roll over before or crow on command.

As we walked from the courthouse, my old man retold and rehashed that story with some pride and he said to me, "Well, son, looks like even though you're always getting in trouble, you also seem to always end up on your feet and up at the head of the class." His words and this entire experience gave my young teenage mind something very powerful to think about: I came to the conclusion that you don't just get in trouble for doing something bad or wrong. You can also get in trouble because you stand up for ideas and principles that challenge people in power. You can get in trouble for exposing the lies and hypocrisy of those who claim to have your best interests at heart. You can earn the anger reserved for those who are so far ahead that people don't realize what you're doing until years later.

Relays

I kept risking my freedom by playing Robin Hood and agitating at every turn. Then one day it all caught up with me. More specifically two police officers finally caught up to me. They were both Harlem cops, African American men, and they knew the streets and knew how to catch me. These two officers of the law took me aside, slapped me around the head, and told me I was on a one-way ticket to jail if I wasn't careful. Even at fifteen, the thought of juvie was enough to send a chill down my spine. Once it was clear that they had my attention, they also told me that the neighborhood was buzzing—not just about my antics but about my speed.

It was through these police officers that I was given the opportunity to train at the New York Pioneer Club, one of the finest track and field clubs in New York. To train at the Pioneer Club was to enter a space where resources and equipment were everywhere and poverty was something that was kept outside the front door. The Pioneer Club also had a traveling team and we went all over the city to compete against other clubs. We were unstoppable, and even with precious little experience or technique, I blew people's minds with my speed. I had never even thought about running for my school because my grades were so terrible and no one ever encouraged me to do anything other than to make as little a ruckus as possible. Besides, the thought of running track for Machine and Metal Trades High School didn't really send my pulse racing. I wasn't exactly Mr. School Spirit.

The Pioneer Club fed my competitive and athletic jones, but I didn't see it leading anywhere. I didn't imagine going to college or even securing my high school diploma. I still dreamed of the Olympics, but didn't know how kicking behinds for the Pioneer Club could possibly lead to running on an international stage. I had no idea how to actually take the next step, and at fifteen, I was hardly getting a great deal of guidance.

Then a whole bunch of broken bones dramatically changed my future. Fortunately, none of those broken bones were mine. I had a very good buddy on the high school track team named Stanley Meacham. Stanley broke his arm and came to me, his arm in a cast, with a pleading look on his face and said, "Carlos, everyone knows you're making waves with the Pioneer Club. Now we need another guy for the relay team." I had no desire to do this whatsoever. Our high school team was nothing special at all. It had no status and no buzz. But Stanley was my friend, so I tried to say it as nicely as possible and even "shine" him a little bit. "Well, my man, you broke your arm, it's not like you broke your leg," I said. "If you broke your leg, then maybe I'd step up. But if you really cared about this team, then you'd run with one arm." He looked at me and laughed and said, "Alright, Carlos, I'm going to run with this cast on, but I'll remember what you said."

He did remember. He remembered when by sheer divine—or demonic—intervention another member of the track team, Victor Vasquez, broke his leg. Now I was stuck. I still had zero interest in running for this team, but I had given my word that I would try to help if they were in a pinch. I agreed to at least check out a practice and see if it was as bare bones as I feared it would be. As it turned out, the practice wasn't as bare bones as I feared. It was worse.

The school didn't have its own track, which wasn't a surprise. More surprising was that we didn't even have access to a public track. Instead the team had to put in its practice time on the unforgiving concrete of the boardwalk. As bad as that was, when it rained the practice situation was even worse. On the rainy or snowy days the team would take all the tables in the cafeteria and push them up against the walls, then open up the cafeteria doors and run down the hall and through the cafeteria. But first of course we had to make sure there weren't globs of ketchup or liquid on the floor that could cause any nasty spills during sprints. Yes, that was the workout area. The cafeteria. I thought it was amateur hour.

At first, as I watched the team line up and train on the boardwalk, my thinking was that I had the Pioneer Club and that was more than enough for me. But when the coach, a very mild-mannered gentleman named Mr. Youngerman, asked everyone to line up for the 100-yard dash, it was like a current of electricity went involuntarily through my body. I loved the 100-yard dash. Loved it. The coach wanted every last member of the team to line up so he could see who really had the jets on his team. I didn't have my track shoes with me on that day. I hadn't shown up to run so I was wearing these big, heavy, clodhoppers. We called them "Ivy League shoes" because they had no style. Normally I cared a great deal about looking sharp, but my father, remember, was a shoemaker and for him, when it came to your feet, style meant nothing. In his mind, if you had on Ivy League shoes, you were good to go because they would never wear out on the broken asphalt of New York City and so that's what all my brothers, my sister, and I would wear.

Despite these Ivy League shoes, I lined up alongside the fastest guys on the high school team in my street clothes and my clodhoppers to run 100 yards. When the coach said "go," I pumped my legs, and felt the resistance against my pants. I kicked out my feet and felt the heaviness of my shoes. And then, I crossed the finish line and saw that everyone else was way back, snacking on my dust. Mild-mannered Mr. Youngerman whooped loudly and said, "Oh, shit, we got a phenom here."

I liked my teammates and felt good being appreciated for something that was connected to my school, so I decided to run the citywide indoor season. Mr. Youngerman immediately put me on the relay team and I was ready to do my thing. But as we got under way, I came to realize that I was about as competitive a performer as existed on that team. I didn't know I had that kind of fire inside of me. I first noticed it when it started to bother me that Mr. Youngerman, once again a very nice man, didn't know too much about track and field, which, if you're a track coach, is a bit of a problem. He also didn't see winning the race as particularly important, which, for a track coach, is also a bit of a problem. Before one meet, Mr. Youngerman took us in the back of the stadium and told us, "Listen, guys, I don't expect you fine young boys to do anything special. You just go out there and have some fun because you know you guys can't really beat these guys. Best to just put in a good showing and call it a day." Not exactly Al Pacino in *Any Given Sunday.*

On one level, no doubt, what Mr. Youngerman was saying was true. Our school hadn't won a damn thing up to that point. We were the sorry Machine and Metal Trades High School team practicing in a cafeteria, and everyone in the city knew it. But when your own coach says that he doesn't expect you to do anything and you look around at your teammates and they are actually nodding their heads while he's speaking, you find out mighty fast whether or not you have a fire in your belly. In other words, I was really, really, pissed off. I blew up. "What do you mean, you don't expect us to do anything?" I yelled. "Well why are we out here? I'm out here to win. And anyone here who didn't show up to win needs to get back on that damn bus." I almost told coach he had forty-eight hours to get it together! Instead,

I turned to the team, and said, "Listen up, now. Y'all get the baton close enough, get it in my hands, and we're going to be alright." It was time to take it to the track.

When we walked into the stadium from the locker room, the crowd was thrumming like only a New York City track event at that time in history could. All the powerhouse schools competing had cheerleaders singing and chanting about how they were going to win all the races. There were cheerleaders and cheering sections from Boys High and DeWitt Clinton in particular. Everyone had a fight song and everyone was going nuts except for our school. Nobody knew or cared about Machine and Metal Trades High School. We had no cheering section, no fight song, and no attention. I'll never forget—our team was so stunned watching the speed with which the other teams were warming up and running practice sprints that we were forgetting to stretch and warm up ourselves. In our eyes, the other teams looked like they didn't have legs. It looked like they had wheels and were just "rolling" up and down the tracks.

I could see the pained apprehension in the eyes of my teammates, so I gathered them around and said the most obvious thing that came into my mind. "They only look fast because they're running and we're not!" I don't know why, but it sounded smart at the time. At least it loosened our guys up so we could take time to warm up properly. When it was our turn to run some practice sprints, the glee clubs and cheerleaders quickly went from dogging us to silence. No one had heard of us, and we were rolling in a way that sent people's eyes popping. We rolled so fast up and down the track that people in the crowd decided to make up their own fight song for Machine and Metal Trades. We were like the track equivalent of Rocky or Rudy or any little engine that could.

Granted the improvised fight song wasn't exactly music to remember, but we were now in the mix. We had stepped up. We had some status. When the actual races started, our confidence was sky-high and we simply blew those other boys away. I particularly had made quite the splash, and it earned me an invite to the Penn Relays.

For those who don't know, the Penn Relays are the oldest and most prestigious track and field event in the United States. From 1895, when it was known as the Penn Relays Carnival, getting called to run in the Penn Relays was like being called up to play in the Major Leagues. Thousands of people from all over the world would be racing and watching, and if I ever dreamed of running in the Olympics, making the right kind of impression at the Penn Relays would be an absolutely essential task.

There is absolutely no slacking on your game at the Penn Relays. I was ready to run and ready to be known. There was just one problem: if I was running in the Penn Relays, I needed real track and field spikes. Ivy League clodhoppers were certainly not going to cut it. Ordinary sneakers were not going to cut it either.

I was always the type of kid who would sooner walk through hell in a gasoline suit than ask my mother and father for any kind of money. I was always working and if I wasn't working, I was hustling. Either way, my thoughts were always about trying to make my own way.

When I was younger, opening the doors at the Savoy and singing songs for the swells, sometimes I would come home and my pockets would be so fat that my father would ask me for a loan. But I knew that if I was really going to compete at the Penn Relays, having proper spikes was nonnegotiable. Since I wouldn't ask my parents for money, I took the next best option. I went and took all the money I had saved up and played the numbers. The numbers were like the down-low lotto. You would place money on a combination of numbers and if they came up, you would get a hefty payback. The people who ran the numbers rackets in Harlem were the sharpest dressed cats in town, with big cars that made your jaw drop. Well, the reason their clothes and rides were so nice was because the numbers were a game you were made to lose. Many a person in Harlem lost their paychecks playing the numbers.

On this particular day, you could count me as one of them. Yes, there's a reason they call it gambling. I missed my numbers and lost it all. I got the news sitting on the shoeshine stand in my father's shop, and must have looked about as dejected and downtrodden as I ever have in my life. My old man looked at me and said, "What's the matter, Johnny?" I said, "I have a problem, Pop. You know the Penn Relays are in just a few days and I need a pair of proper spikes. I tried to take my savings and hit the numbers, but they didn't come up and now I'm here with this opportunity, but if I don't have my spikes, I might as well run in bare feet."

I thought my daddy would be angry at me for betting the numbers and honestly I felt like I deserved whatever he wanted to dish out. But this man could always surprise me. He was quiet for a moment and then he said, "Well, how much do they cost?" I said I didn't know exactly, but it didn't matter since I didn't have a cent to my name. Then this hard-working man just gave me a pinch of bills and told me to go get my spikes. I couldn't believe it. I sprinted out of my daddy's shop, went down to the store that sold secondhand athletic supplies and bought the cheapest spikes I could find. That was all we had money for, but I was glad to have them. They were so heavy, so old, and so creased, they looked like the spikes that Jesse Owens wore at the 1936 Olympics. They had these long spikes and were made out of an old heavy leather from a cow that might have been wrangled by Billy the Kid. That's what we could afford so that's what I had. I may have been wearing a Smithsonian exhibit on my feet, but having spikes officially put me in the game and I was ready to take on the Penn Relays.

The marquee event of the Penn Relays was of course the relays. On my particular team, I had another coach dedicated to the anti-pep talk. He said, "While I don't expect you guys to win anything, let's go for fifth place. If you're in fifth place, hold onto fifth place. And if you can't make fifth place, just get out there and have a good time." I stood up and said, "Man, I'm not traveling all the way from New York on no train to go to Philadelphia and not come home with something. I'm going to get something to come back with." I gathered the guys on my squad around me and told them, "Look, fellas, I'm going to run anchor. If we're even 15 yards behind the lead man, and you pass me the baton, we will win this race. Just stay within 15 and I promise you we will win."

We were gearing up to make some noise and my team was excited before the start. But excitement and adrenaline only gets you so far and when they handed me the stick for the anchor leg I must have been at least 25 yards behind the lead man. I didn't care. I hit a gear I had never felt before and just started rolling by every person in front of me. All I had to do was just try to get around a beanpole white kid from Little Rock, Arkansas. He looked like he might've been six five, six six, and skinny as a rail. He was clearly a smart runner, too because when we hit the backstretch, he used his size and stride to keep me back. I would try and pass him and sneak by him on the inside, and then he would jump in front of me and I would have to drop my kick and double-kick and then drop backward a step, then kick and double-kick again to get by him. When I would break outside, he'd move outside. When we were finally coming off the last turn and ready to hit that final straightaway, there was no more space for tricks and I was close enough to turn him into toast. I jumped and said, "You can't stop my ass now." And I blew by him. I was about maybe 10 yards, 15 yards from the tape clear sailing, and, man, I was rolling. I can see the finish line and I know we're going to win this thing and the crowd is roaring in my ears. Then all of a sudden, the dream became a nightmare. My entire body became shocked by rigor mortis from head to toe. It felt like somebody dropped a piano off the fifteenth floor and it landed on my body. In track and field, this is actually more common than you might think. They call it "the Bear." Well, on this particular day, "the Bear" jumped on my back and clawed my every nerve ending.

"The Bear" had never happened to me in my entire athletic life. I didn't know if I was dying or what. I just hit the ground and I remember grabbing the gravel on the track in my hand and letting that shit slide through my fingers. Only the tips of my thumbs could even move. As I was lying prone, locked up by "the Bear," guys were hurdling over me trying to get to the tape. That's the agony of defeat right there. As I lay there, every muscle locked together, only one thought was going through my head. I said to myself, "Man, the hell with this. I ain't never running track no more." I was in pain, but I wasn't embarrassed as much as I was bewildered. How could this happen to me? Teammates and friends ran out of the stands to see if I was all right and I heard the trainer and some of the coaches and runners say, "The Bear jumped on Carlos! Carlos was caught by the bear!" I didn't even know what that meant. Who is this bear and why did it jump on me?

Eventually, after a serious stretch and rubdown, I was able to pull myself off the track. In my head, I was imagining limping off into the sunset and returning to a normal life of robbing trains. But when I trudged back into the stands, people mobbed me and were giving me a whole different kind of respect. Everybody was telling me, "Man, you were running with the kind of speed that you only see in the Olympics. If you didn't fall down with fifteen strides to go, you could've broke a world record!" Coaches and trainers were also surrounding me. They didn't even care about "the Bear" and how the race ended. They were jazzing on the potential I showed. I was also jazzed.

The whole experience was a wake-up call to me that track and field could be my ticket to the Olympic Games. But it also put me on notice that there was an art to this. It wasn't just about running as fast as your legs could carry you. This is especially the case when you sprint any kind of distance greater than 100 meters. For instance, as the coaches observing the Penn Relays kept pointing out to me, I could run the straightaway like an Olympian, but when it came time for me to make the turn, I had a habit of swinging my body all the way out to the far edge of the track. My form was so primitive, I would use my right hand like a fan, flapping it up and down, to keep my balance on turns. In many of these early races, I'd eventually win, but the pattern would be me blowing them away on the first straightaway, losing my lead on the turn, and then catching up and winning on that last straightaway. That approach might work against high school competition, but if I was going to make it to the next level, I needed technique, I needed focus, I needed serious training. I was tired of people saying, "Who is this big dude here? He doesn't know squat about track and field, but he's good." I had never been a quality student in school because of my dyslexia, but I studied the art of how to run a serious race until my eyes bled. You can't overstate how important it is as a young man to get positive reinforcement. I never had a teacher say, "If you just applied yourself, you could make it in academics. You have all the potential in the world." But I did have coaches voicing those sentiments to me about track. It felt better than any hustle.

I was ready to learn and I did just that. Once I had my technique down, I was now ready to add a little flair. Success was one thing, but I knew from the streets of Harlem that you made a name for yourself with a little bit of flair. I am very surprised when people look at these modern athletes like Terrell Owens and Chad Ochocinco like they were the first athletes to ever have some spice in their game. When I was issued my first official, top-of-the-line cotton sweats, the first thing I did was get a magic marker and write a *J* and a *C* on each half of my behind. When I wore the sweats in warm-ups, I'd make a point to speed past the competition so they'd get those letters in their heads: J, C, J, C, J, C, J, C. Everybody wanted to know who the hell is this guy JC? Does he think he's Jesus Christ? And I'd say, "Well almost. But I'm just John Carlos." This was how you built a reputation. But there was no building a reputation without getting the skills down first.

I was feeling at the top of my game, winning races and getting a great deal of praise along the way. I wasn't even out of high school at this point, but I felt like a full-grown man. It was at this point in my life when in very short order, I entered a relationship and—faster, it seemed, than I could run my wind sprints—I was married. It was 1963. I was relaxing down by the public pool with my buddies and one of the people in my crew was making fun of me because I had an eye for the ladies and he told me that I would never settle down. He said I'd be like one of those old playboys, hitting on younger ladies when I had a head full of gray. I shot right back at him that the next woman I saw walking through the ladies changing area would be my wife. We were laughing, but we were also looking, just in case. Then, wouldn't you know, through those doors walked Karen Benjamin Groce. I found out soon enough that everyone called her Kim. Kim was beautiful, kind, and somewhat fragile. I wanted to care for her and be the man in her life. Eighteen months later on February 29, 1965, we were married. No coincidence, but it was a week after Malcolm was assassinated. I felt this urge to move forward, to grow up, to be my own man. My head was twisted with emotion at the time.

Even back then you didn't see too many people get married in high school, especially when there weren't any "buns in the oven," so to speak. People were breaking our eardrums, screeching, "You guys are too young! You don't have to do this!" Maybe they were right, but at the time that meant nothing to us. I wanted to be married because I felt like I could handle the responsibility and more importantly, with the values I had, I believed that getting married was the only way I could possibly be my own man. Every time I would stand up to Old Earl Carlos, his response would always be, "I'm the captain of this ship." I had no response for that. It's true. He was the captain of the ship. Well, I felt like I needed my own ship. The older I became, the more I found myself disagreeing with my family, the more our little apartment was just getting too small for me. It made perfect sense to me that I needed to get my own family and I needed to get my own pad.

Kim and I were married on that chilly February day in a neighborhood Harlem church, right down the street from my junior high school. I remember she had her wedding gown on and I had my tux on and when the wedding was over, we strutted—tux and wedding dress—right by our high school. All my boys and all the girls saw us and hooted and hollered. They loved it and we were dancing on clouds.

Once we were married, we needed to figure out a way to make a life. I was still finishing high school and making waves on the amateur track circuit. But Kim had a very good job as a personal secretary for an established family in Harlem. We were able to secure our own little apartment in the Bronx as well as secure our own precious little life. That November, our beautiful little girl, Kimme, was born. Kim made that name up. It all felt so right. I remember looking at Kimme for the first time and saying "That's my baby." It looked like smooth sailing for the Carlos family. Looking back, it was much more like the calm before the hurricane.

Three

■　■　■　■

Trouble in Texas

I kept winning races in record-setting fashion across the region, with the opposition helpless to do more than read the JC on my backside. Big-time colleges and universities started showing up at meets, sending letters to our house, and making on-the-table offers of scholarships and under-the-table offers as well. At the time, my eyes were squarely on taking my new family to California and the schools of California had their eyes on me. Cali was the unquestioned mecca of track and field, and I heard from UCLA, USC, Berkeley, and the place known as Speed City, San Jose State. But our mutual interest was hit by a sudden and brutal rigor mortis, like it was attacked by "the Bear," when the schools saw my academic transcripts. You didn't need a particularly impressive grade point average to get an athletic scholarship, but I didn't even meet that standard. At the time, people didn't know or care what dyslexia was. I didn't know either. I just knew that I had terrible trouble with my studies and I thought school was the problem. I had never given a spare thought toward my academics and I gave even less of a thought about going to college. In addition to track and field, all I had devoted myself to was hustling money, and on that front, I had graduated with honors. But not until very late did I see the long game. I never thought college would be my future so when they came calling, I just didn't have it together. I wasn't the first star athlete with terrible grades and some schools made clear that they were willing to bend a rule or two to get me on campus, but when on top of my transcripts, they heard that I was married with a child, their interest dried up like a shallow puddle in the Arizona desert. UCLA was the most honorable school that approached me. They wanted to offer me a scholarship, but first see me go to a junior college and work on my grades. But I was impatient and stubborn. I also felt like I was much smarter than my grades demonstrated. I was a child of Harlem, of Malcolm, and of a generation that wasn't going to accept second-class citizenship. That approach to the world, in all honesty, meant that there were times that people were saying things that I wasn't trying to hear.

I told everyone, "Man, I ain't going to no junior college." But that meant when high school ended, I was an athlete without a home.

That changed when I competed in what was called an "all-comers" track meet in New Jersey. This was an open invitational, and true to form, I had everyone snacking on my dust. At the meet, there was another runner named Pete Peterson. He was a young, hip, white student at East Texas State University, a school I really didn't know existed. Back then, looking back, the divisions were really was less about black and white than they were generational. I liked Peterson. We spoke at great length and Peterson must have been a smooth talker because he really sold me on coming to East Texas. After talking it up, we went to the administrative office of the track meet and on the spot he called the school's head track coach, Delmer Brown. Right in front of me, Peterson said, "There is a runner here, Johnny Carlos, that says he's not going to school anywhere, and this kid is a monster." That was enough for Delmer Brown, who knew my name and reputation, and he offered me a full ride on the spot. Hearing that a coach like Delmer Brown wanted me without conditions was enough for me as well.

I knew that Delmer Brown had worked as a trainer with the 1964 US Track and Field Olympic team. That team included one of my heroes, "Bullet" Bob Hayes, who tied the world record in the 100-meter dash, and then shocked the world with a sub-nine anchor leg in the 4x100 relays. Anyone who was just one degree away from Bob Hayes was someone I wanted to be my coach.

I wanted to go to East Texas, but I was mindful—always mindful—of being exploited, so I wanted something back. When Coach Brown offered me a full ride, I made clear that certain things would have to be done to take care of my family. I didn't care if this was above board or below board. I didn't care if we were bending the rules or breaking them. The fact is that the terms of any athletic scholarship are fundamentally exploitative, no matter how sanctified by the NCAA. I would make damn sure that I would get the best possible deal I could.

I made clear to Coach Brown that I wanted Kim to have a job in East Texas waiting for her so my family could build its nest egg. I made clear, and this was nonnegotiable, that Kim and baby Kimme could get free transportation to every track meet, no matter how far away, so we could stay a tight family unit. I also had questions about the racism that my family might have to face in East Texas. Honestly, what I knew about Texas couldn't have filled a single page. I knew that I didn't hear about big civil rights struggles down there, but that could mean either that there were no problems or it could mean that people were too scared to fight back. Coach Brown and his assistants assured me that Texas would be safe harbor for my beautiful black family. They said with straight faces, "Texas isn't like Alabama or Mississippi. There's no prejudice here. We're right near the big city of Dallas. We don't see color in East Texas. Your wife and kids will be able to eat wherever they want, stay wherever they want, sit wherever they want on the bus, go to all the track meets, and see you run no matter where we go."

It sounded so nice and it sounded so true coming out of their mouths. But it was about the farthest thing from the truth, from top to bottom and from A to Z. I don't think they were deliberately trying to mislead me, but I do think there is a cautionary lesson here. If you are ever in a position where you are assessing whether or not a place is afflicted by racism, it's best not to ask older white folks for the definitive perspective. For example, Coach Brown and his assistants left out the fact that East Texas State had only even been integrated for one year. It was certainly true that East Texas State was located only about 65 miles northeast of Dallas, but in the mid-1960s, it was not just 65 miles from big D. It was also about 65 years in the past from Dallas, if you feel me.

But the Carlos family had committed to East Texas so we packed up our bags and made our way far from home and back into the past. It didn't take long to realize that we had entered a time machine. In fact, as soon as we landed at the airport, I realized that we might have made a terrible mistake. Imagine that feeling: being a teenage father, trying to be a man, picking up your whole family and taking them from Harlem, USA, to East Texas, getting off that plane, and seeing right away that this was not a healthy or positive move. Both of our families and all our friends told us that I should just go by myself and leave my wife and child back in New

York City and send for them later if it was good. If it wasn't good, we'd spend holidays and summers together. Maybe that should have been the strategy, but my wife said, "If you go, we go. We're a team."

I liked the sound of that. Yes. We are a team. But then we landed at the airport, and I saw that Team Carlos was more like Team Tecumseh and we were surrounded by cowboys. This was many years before the big Dallas–Ft. Worth International Airport was built. There was just one small terminal shaped like a box with a bronze statue of a Texas Ranger right in the middle. Then over the bronze Ranger's shoulder, we both saw something that we'd just read about in the newspapers or heard about from relatives: bathrooms marked "White" and "Colored." I couldn't help it. I told Kim to wait a moment with Kimme and I walked into the white bathroom to have a look. It was about as clean and shiny as the operating room of a hospital. Then I used the "colored" bathroom and it was about as nasty as a New York back alley. There was running water on the floor and the toilets looked like they hadn't been cleaned since the Alamo. I remember standing on that wet floor and thinking, "Uh oh. We might have ourselves a serious problem."

When I left the bathroom, Coach Delmer Brown was there to greet us and I heard him lecturing to Kim in a loud voice, "Yup! You have your bathroom space for whites and coloreds. But it don't mean anything." Then we took that 65-mile journey back in time to the location of East Texas State, a town called Commerce, Texas. Over that 65-mile stretch, my name seemed to magically change. I wasn't John Carlos anymore. I was "boy" or "son." Or I was "that Negro feller." The first time I heard that, I didn't hear "Negro." You say "Negro" with a thick southern accent, and it sounds an awful lot like "Nigra." And when I heard "Nigra," I thought it was another word that in Harlem would get you an ass-whupping on general principle.

I rolled up my sleeves ready to beat this random person in the head and Kim, who could be iron tough when she had to be, stepped in front of me and put some vise grips on my arms and said, "No, Johnny, I don't think he called you that. He called you something else." Kim had this ability to calm me down and cool my temper like nobody else, and at that moment she saved me from a world of grief.

My young wife may have kept me from blowing my top, but I already knew sure as day that I had made a mistake. Toto, this wasn't Harlem anymore. But what could I do? I had already told my family, Kim's family, and all our friends that I was going to be a man and take my wife and daughter to Texas and build our own life. I wasn't going to call mommy and daddy and whine, "I made a mistake, send money for us so we can go home!" So my wife and I took several deep breaths, and agreed to make a home for ourselves in Commerce. But every last shred of dignity that we took with us to Texas was challenged.

First that sweet job promised to my wife by Coach Brown, so we could build our nest egg, had disappeared upon our arrival. I actually threatened to quit the team over that little lie, and then it magically materialized. But not everything did. The free transportation that they promised would be there for Kim and Kimme to see me run in all my track meets, was just a bald-faced lie. We had to pay out of pocket to travel together as a family when I had away meets. This wasn't something we could afford, and just as I feared, our inevitable separation put a strain on Kim and our family.

Then there was the day our beautiful little toddler Kimme was out scampering around in our neighborhood playground having a fine old time playing with another little girl who happened to be white. They were just having a blast because kids don't know a damn thing about prejudice, racism, or none of that. That has to be taught to kids, drilled into their heads. Sure enough, the little girl's father came storming toward them and yelled at his daughter, "Don't you ever play with this little nigger girl again!" I don't think my daughter had a clue as to what he said as much as how he said it: with that special kind of anger we hadn't heard up in Harlem. The way he said it, with a kind of wicked rage, just frightened the holy heck out of her. She came running toward me, crying, her nose running, shaking, and hysterical over what had just happened. I felt the old rage and went out there to deal with it. My neighbors, my wife, and, I suppose, my sense of self-preservation kept me from beating him into the ground like a railroad spike, but I made it clear to him that if this ever happened again, his time on this earth would be painful and brief.

The aftermath of this incident gave me another insight into the realities of where we were living. We had experienced this big racial to-do in my neighborhood, and instead of this racist fool being the lightning rod of criticism and scorn, it was the Carlos family who were the troublemakers. It was just a terrible situation. Not only did people cut my family and me a wide berth, but there were more than a few black folks in our community who asked me why I even got so upset! I'm not sure today people realize how deep that divide was between Southern "Negroes" and Northern black people. I wasn't going to take a teaspoon of what I called "that nonsense." But to Southern Negroes, "that nonsense" was just daily life and most in East Texas were just numb to it.

I tried to look outside our neighborhood to the other black students to see if there was any support we could get so we wouldn't be all alone on this island that our neighbors had created around us. But if this was the era of student revolt, it somehow took a sharp detour around East Texas State. Most of the students at the school, black and white, were from that immediate area. An outsider was somebody from *West* Texas, let alone someone from Harlem. The attitude of most of the black students was made very clear to Kim and me: "I'm not going to rock the boat and you shouldn't either. The way things are in East Texas is simply the way things are." Here I am with a young family, wanting to be captain of my own ship like Earl Carlos, and I'm being told to not rock the boat.

"Don't have a social life with anyone but black people," they told us. Privately, they told me, "Don't even think of talking with any white women if no one else is around." And the advice that I thought came out of a history book but was right there in my face: "Stay in your place, speak when spoken to." It was very frightening because, unspoken, were the consequences if I didn't stay in line. I'm not even talking about vigilante violence or lynching or anything like that. They just handed out ninety-nine-year prison sentences to black folks like it was nothing. Another guy went to jail because he could not feed his family, and he stole some bread and bologna. He went to jail for sixty-five years. That's what was happening all around us. Every prison sentence held a threat.

The coaching staff and administration at East Texas State weren't exactly sources of support either. Coach Delmer Brown and I had a very short honeymoon. Our differences became apparent immediately because he was just not accustomed to having a guy like me coming down to Texas from New York with attitudes and opinions about every last thing he was doing. I guess he thought I was going to just fall in and be like everybody else and just bow, scrape, and give allegiance to whatever his attitudes about track and field—or even the larger world—happened to be. Coach Brown put up with me because I was dominating across the state. I put up with him because I didn't have a choice, but the tension simmered and occasionally boiled over.

One spring, Coach Brown wanted us running up and down the stadium steps. If you've never had the pleasure of running stadium steps, please be assured that you are not missing anything. It's the kind of drill that you feel in your legs for hours afterwards. I thought that doing this kind of high-impact drill was a mistake considering that we had a huge conference meet the next day. In addition we would be caravanning to the conference meet in a couple of cramped station wagons, which would be making our legs stiff and sore anyways. In those days, we never flew anywhere and on that East Texas budget, we never went on the bus. It was station wagons all the time. I thought that doing stairs was just too damn much running to get in a station wagon and drive for half a day the next day.

Being a little older, and because I won so many of my races, people on the team started to look at me as a leader. I told everyone on the team, "Man, I'm not running those stairs. I'll start, but then you'll see me jog. And then you'll see me walk. And if Coach Brown doesn't like to see me walk those stairs, then that's just tough."

Coach Brown noticed when I went from running to jogging but didn't say anything. He just stewed. I saw that very pale face get awfully red. By the time I was walking, Coach lost it. He was so pissed off, he started walking toward me, cussing at me, calling me every bad name in the book. I just stared back at him like he wasn't worth a single solitary second of my time. Then, I don't know what possessed him, but he picked up a hammer and started swinging it around like he was going to do me some kind of bodily harm. Everybody was officially freaking out.

Fortunately, Coach Brown's son Danny was there helping with practice. Danny was good people. I looked over and I said "Danny, you better come down here and take that toy from your father before he gets himself hurt." Well, as soon as things settled down, I decided that I'd had enough.

I took off my shorts and jock right there on the field and threw it right in his face and said, "You think you can take out a hammer when you don't get your way? Well, I'm done, I'm finished." Then I went up and I took all my stuff out of my locker and threw it on the ground and I went and got in the shower. I know Danny must have said something to his father, because while I was showering, Coach Brown walked in and tried to make amends. But at that point, I was so enormously pissed off that I told him, "Delmer, I don't want to hear nothing you have to say. Get out of here or I might whip your behind buck naked right in this shower. *Leave!*"

I remember storming out of the locker room. Later that day, I was in front of the student body association's student union building, holding court, saying in a loud voice that I was gone. It became like an impromptu speak-out and I was speechifying about racism, sports, and Texas. I said I was gone. I said that I was nobody's mule and that my family would be getting our things together and leaving town on the next plane.

But then, every assistant coach on the track team approached me while I was talking and tried to talk me out of leaving. This had a bigger effect on me than you might think. That's the thing about sports sometimes. I said to them I refused to be subservient, but, as they told me, I was also the best athlete and the fastest runner that they had on the team. They said I had an obligation to my teammates and that cut me to the quick. Honestly, as great as Muhammad Ali, Billie Jean King, and Arthur Ashe were, I will always have a different kind of respect for people like Bill Russell and Jim Brown because I know from experience how hard it is to not only be a rebel but to have to face down that charge that you are somehow letting down your team by expressing your views. Later my views would evolve on this question, but at the time, I couldn't let the team down and agreed to come back.

After this incident, Coach Brown had a much different posture toward me. He would always step around me with a cautious sense that he wouldn't communicate with me unless he absolutely had to. I would describe it like Coach Brown was tiptoeing through raindrops. He definitely didn't want to be seen as having caved to me, or even worse, as an ally who had somehow been converted to standing in my corner supporting my every grievance. He also, even more importantly, didn't want me to get pissed off and leave the team. It was a precarious situation and almost every week, it seemed like it might just blow up. Every time this happened, it was the team that acted as Coach Brown's savior.

After one particularly ugly confrontation, when once again I was ready to walk, the entire team sat down with me for a players-only meeting. There were some white guys on our team who fought for civil rights and knew where I was coming from, and backed my frustrations more than most of the black students on campus. They made clear that they had my back but that we would not be able to make the situation for the next generation of athletes any more just if I decided to up and quit. I had this one friend on the team, who happened to be white, Terry Barnett, who passed away in 2010. Terry was pure gold. He wore his support for civil rights and his antiracism like a badge of honor. Terry taught me that the fight for social justice was a marathon not a sprint. In that meeting, Terry and the fellas took pains to let me know that they understood my frustrations with East Texas and Coach Brown but that we had a bond that was more important than all of that nonsense. Terry had me imagining that this team of new jack rebels could really win the Lone Star Conference if I stayed. We could make a statement that a multiracial, civil-rights-supporting team could put all the nonsense aside and accomplish something. I had never felt more a part of something as these young men stared at me with that intense kind of hope that only sports, in my experience, can provide.

I was standing there remembering how in high school my coach was just happy to be invited to the tournaments and now here was a group that not only wanted to win, but was looking to my rebellious self to lead the way. I loved the attitude and I told them that this was the best moment I'd had since coming to East Texas. I said, "Damn right I'll stay. We're going to win this thing. We can really do it!"

I remember walking up to the chalkboard and writing it down: I scrawled in big letters both personal and team predictions. I wrote that at the decisive Lone Star Conference meets, I was going to win the 100, and the 200, and that we were going to win the sprint relay, the mile relay, and the whole nine yards. We were whooping it up and I felt like I was finally home.

But then in walked Coach Delmer Brown to all this united madness. Coach Brown, instead of being more positive for his team, looked at all the predictions written up on the chalkboard, and still trying to tiptoe through raindrops with me, tried to capture the mood of the room and failed miserably.

"How are you going to possibly beat some of these guys on these other squads?" he asked. "They're tops! We just have to take it one race at a time." I think on one level, he was trying to coddle me by setting the bar so low, so that I'd feel no pressure and would be more likely to stay. But all he did was kill the buzz in the room. Finally I said, "If I say I'm going to beat somebody and if we say we're going to win this conference coach, you need to support us 5,000 percent. But you look like you're telling this team we're not going to beat the opposition."

I committed to stay, and sure enough we won the 1967 Lone Star Conference title. Actually, we slam-dunked it. But the relationship with

Coach Brown from that point on was always the same: it was always getting worse. Everything he did rubbed me the wrong way. I especially couldn't handle how Coach Brown would talk about us to other coaches and to the press. I'll never forget when we had a major meet in Brownsville, Texas, and Coach Brown was woofing to the other coaches and said, "My horses are going to beat all the other horses out there." To put it mildly, this was not all right with me. I had made the decision that I would put up with a great deal. But I was a man. My teammates were men. People might call us boy or son, but for damn sure, we were nobody's horses. I took Coach Brown aside and said, "Hello, coach. It's John Carlos the Horse. Nice to meet you." He froze because he knew I'd heard him. I then said, "This horse has a brain and the power of speech and doesn't feel like running the mile relay today, no thank you." Coach Brown lost his temper and fired back that if I wasn't down with his plan, I could get dressed and leave. I think he was bluffing, but I wasn't.

After my street clothes were on, he ran up to me and got in my face, calling me all kinds of names. No more dancing between raindrops for Coach Brown. I said it straight to him, "Don't put me in no grudge race and call me no damn horse. If you offend me as a man, you aren't going to see me run." Then he ridiculed me in front of the whole team, saying that all my talk of team togetherness and winning the conference title were just that: talk.

I left the meet that day. But when the local paper asked him later why I was in street clothes, he completely flipped and smiled wide and made some nice, pleasant statement in the newspaper about how I had been scratched from the race that day because I was a little gimpy and he was resting me for a future race. I couldn't stop shaking my head over that bit of Texan cow pie. Of course he didn't like me, but he wanted to keep me.

It meant that the BS was always piled high. As they say, it's always bigger in Texas.

Then another rift went down when I received my copy of *Track and Field News* in the mail. The hot story in *Track and Field News* was that there were rumblings of a boycott by African American athletes of the 1968 Olympics in Mexico City. At its heart were two world-class track stars from Speed City itself, San Jose State University: Tommie Smith and Lee Evans. Alongside them was a charismatic San Jose State professor named Dr. Harry Edwards. They were making a very aggressive and very serious argument that to my ears was pure common sense. They said that they couldn't just run in Mexico City, like everything was hunky-dory, when there was so much racism both in the United States Olympic Committee and US society as a whole. They said that they couldn't bring gold and glory to a country where so much of Dr. King's dream was deferred. They said that the individual glory of Olympic stardom had to wait until we had real justice here at home. This to my ears was right on time.

After this issue of *Track and Field News* hit the school, a student reporter for the East Texas State newspaper asked if they could interview me about my thoughts on the possibility of a boycott. I agreed but said I would do it on one condition: that every word out of my mouth would be published exactly as I said it, without creative editing and without a filter.

To his credit, he agreed and we dropped a piece that set our little campus on its ear. The article quoted me saying that even though the Olympics had been my dream since I was a little boy, I would be proud to give it all up for the greater good. I spoke about all my experiences and my family's experiences with racism in East Texas and asked how I could represent a country that had treated me and mine so terribly. I spoke in harsh and unflinching terms about the school, the community, the state of Texas, and the country and made it clear that if I was fortunate enough to be chosen for the US Olympic team, I would support the boycott.

The flames from this story shot up faster than those trees I threw gasoline on all those many years ago to kill the caterpillars. This was a bigger problem than just conflicts between Coach Delmer Brown and me. The Athletic Director Jesse Heathorn took not just me but every black athlete at the school, sat us all in a room, and made it plain that he wouldn't have any of this boycott talk associated with East Texas State. It was funny to me that he just gathered the black athletes when the white cats like Terry were more serious and social justice–minded than many of them. It just showed me how out of touch Heathorn was. He said to us, "Every person in the room has a choice. Love it or leave it." I was ready to leave it. But the straw that broke my back was still to come.

I had two teammates who were very dear to me: Don Mitchell and Jimmy Ray Smith. The three of us took an anatomy class that was damn near impossible. Anatomy was a subject that in those days before computers and spell-check, required you to not only know the answers but spell every word correctly. These words could run forty to fifty letters each. It was like trying to walk a minefield blindfolded.

I wasn't the best student, but the three of us had other motives for taking the class: our professor was none other than Coach Delmer Brown. We thought that when it came time for our exams, certain liberties would be granted us and it would be a breeze. Brown was also, remember, a trainer on that historic 1964 track and field Olympics team with "Bullet" Bob Hayes, Billy Mills, and Al Oerter. In this class, it would be common for Coach Brown to spend ten minutes on his lesson plan, and then go off on tangents and tell elaborate Texas yarns about how he talked Billy Mills into winning the gold medal in the 10,000 meters, and the mystical ways he turned Bob Hayes into a legend. You really needed a pair of serious boots and maybe a noseclip to get through some of these lectures, but they were nothing if not entertaining.

When the anatomy exam time finally came around, Don and Jimmy Ray were nervous, thinking they had no chance to pass this test. I smiled at Don and Jimmy Ray and said, "Fellas, here is what I'm going to do. For every question on this test, I'm just going to answer with stories about how Coach Brown helped Billy Mills and Bob Hayes since that's what he was flapping his gums about in class."

They told me I was crazy, but that's exactly what I did. Athletic stardom certainly does have its privileges, and I was given a passing grade. Don and Jimmy Ray worked their behinds off studying, but they still failed the exam, and they were stripped of their athletic scholarships. I came to find out that their scholarships were taken away because there were two young track stars in New York whom they wanted to bring onto the team. The scuttlebutt was that they were bringing these New Yorkers in to watchdog me and try and keep me in check. They would be charged with spying on me, muzzling me, and most critically, keeping me from fanning the flames of an Olympic boycott on campus. That didn't sound like any kind of situation I wanted—for my family or for me. Once you don't trust the people around you, whether you're on a team or in a political or religious organization, it's time to move on. That was a Malcolm X lesson right there. This wasn't about backing away from a challenge. It was about, for the first time, not feeling safe. It felt like there was a target on my back and if there is one place you don't want a target on your back, it's Texas.

Clearly I had to get the hell out of Texas. I packed up my family and we went back to New York. East Texas State was an unbelievably difficult, scarring experience, but it was also an education the likes of which changed my life forever. I learned that people would listen to what I had to say about the world because I was a high-performing athlete. I also learned a great deal just by getting out of Harlem and seeing how the rest of the country lived. I learned that Harlem was the exception and not the rule for the United States. In most of the country, I was "son." I was "boy." I sure as hell wasn't captain of my ship.

But I also learned that this condition of white supremacy could change. I saw that some of the younger generation of white teammates were truly my brothers. We're talking about friendships that have lasted a lifetime, made of bonds that can't be broken. The entire East Texas experience was worth it because I got to become brothers for life with a crew of people from all backgrounds: Jay Johnson, Alfred Taylor, Arthur James, Bill Gaines, Fred Williams, Don Mitchell, Jimmy Ray Smith, Chad Brown, Joe Tave, and especially my dear friend Terry Barnett.

I also learned something that I've carried with me to this day about my absolute refusal to be exploited. That was seared into my mind in East Texas. I saw the way my track dominance generated contracts for the coaches, funds for the athletic department, and opened the purse strings of the boosters. I saw up close the way everyone but the people putting the blood, sweat, and tears into the product was paid. That's why to this day, whenever I speak, I advocate for college athletes to get a little piece of the pie.

Every athlete who's on a scholarship helps pad the bank account of that particular institution. Yet while every athlete contributes, not every athlete walks away with a degree. When you're a student athlete, the message is sent from day one that athletics come first. You aren't a student-athlete, you're an athlete-student and you really need to be compensated from the start. Think about a player like Reggie Bush for USC who had his Heisman Trophy stripped away. Think about how many jerseys the school sold with Reggie Bush's name on it. Think about how many people came to Trojans games week after week, month after month, and drank the beer or bought programs at his games. Think about how much television money they pulled in for his games. That's a tremendous amount of money coming to USC based on his three-year tenure there. I sit back and wonder if anyone gave two cents of care toward his degree. I wonder if Reggie Bush was ever encouraged to take some real classes. Today, he's limping around the field. That young man might be out of the game before he's thirty. What's depressing is that the Reggie Bush story is as old as college athletics and only the amounts and stakes have really changed.

I had tasted that kind of exploitation and I was done with it. It was early 1968, and it was time to go home. I didn't know what my next move would be. I didn't know at this point if I would be trying out for the Olympics or boycotting the Olympics, I was just trying to transition my family from a very bad situation. That's where my head was. It was time for this "horse" to ride back to Harlem.

Four

■　　■　　■　　■

1968

We went back to New York City to touch ground and try to develop some kind of strategy as to what the next move in our lives would be. Kim wanted me to find a job and work. I wanted to stay in shape by running in amateur invitationals and hustle money on the side. But the Lord had other plans for me. When we moved back to the big city, a gentleman by the name of Dr. Harry Edwards happened to be visiting at the same time. Harry, as I mentioned, was the lead organizer for this floating idea of an African American boycott of the 1968 Olympics. He was a very charismatic professor and public speaker. He was a former athlete, standing six foot eight inches tall, muscle-bound, decked out in leather and shades, with a motor that just wouldn't quit. Harry was from the tough streets of East St. Louis, and had used his athletic abilities to leverage a doctorate from Cornell. He was still just twenty-six at this time, a peer and a leader.

Harry tracked me down at my mother's house, where I was helping her with some painting, and said that there was a meeting that night and people were asking if I could attend. The story of supporting the boycott at East Texas State had made its way to Harry's ears and he wanted me involved in the planning. Hearing that there was some actual organizing, that I would be breaking out of my isolation on these issues, was music to my ears. I didn't have to think twice that this was where I needed to be. It was clear to me by that time that Harry was more than someone with style and the power to shock the press. He was a very committed individual who understood and was able to articulate the way racism and athletics mixed.

Harry had a great deal of courage, in my eyes, to even consider an attempt to challenge racism in society from within the world of sports. This was not exactly friendly territory. I felt in my heart that at that moment in history, he was an essential person and he was without fear. If you showed Harry any system, any government, or any status quo, he made it his business to get in its face. He also had picked the perfect tactic: the boycott.

The word of the day was boycott and anyone who was either a black athlete or sympathetic to the cause of black athletes was well versed in the arguments on both sides. And it was clear that you couldn't be a bystander in this struggle: Black, white, or brown, we needed to know which side you were on. When it came time to lend support, the color of your skin didn't matter. And as I learned in East Texas, this was a struggle that was really far more generational than it was racial.

You had a lot of the elder African American "statesmen" and mainstream civil rights leaders hating this kind of plan. You had the older athletes, like Jesse Owens, shocked that we would even consider such a thing. You also had young Caucasian individuals like the rowers from Harvard University lending us some serious support. The movement had gained steam because in February 1968 the president of the IOC, Avery Brundage, the man who delivered the 1936 Olympics to Hitler's Germany, readmitted apartheid South Africa to the Olympic community—as if that racist state had somehow reformed. It gave us focus, energy, and a very clear demand to put on the table: if South Africa was in, we were out. This was the movement, as I knew from the pages of *Track and Field News*. This was what I wanted to be a part of. And this was why I was thrilled when the telephone rang in my mother's apartment, and it was Harry Edwards extending an invite.

Harry told me over the phone that the meeting was taking place downtown at the Americano Hotel. It doesn't even exist anymore, but back then the Americano Hotel used to be right across from the old Madison Square Garden. I would have run out of the door and just left my dust behind, but I did at least have the manners to turn to my mother and ask her if she needed me to finish this paint job or if I could go. She looked at me, saw the fever in my eyes, and told me to just get my behind out of the house.

I recall going down to the Americano that evening, walking into the lobby and being just overwhelmed by the size of it all. I had never really made time in the downtown hotels and my eyes almost popped out of my head. It looked like a movie set, with 50-foot-high ceilings, gaudy chandeliers, and the kind of deep, smoky woodwork that looked like it had been carved and sanded for kings. Honestly, I thought I'd turn the corner and bump into John Dillinger. I gathered myself and I went up to the room where the meeting was to take place.

When I entered that room, I had no expectations whatsoever as to who might be at the meeting or anything of the sort. I just knew it would be the place to be to talk boycott. Other than Harry Edwards, I had no idea who would be there or why. When I walked in, I was immediately shocked to see some of the social-movement political giants that I had seen on television—Andrew Young for one, and Ralph Abernathy, the number two man of the Southern Christian Leadership Conference (SCLC). I was thinking to myself that I couldn't possibly get in trouble with my parents for walking out on that paint job because the SCLC could do no wrong in our household. I was already feeling like gold and awestruck around Abernathy and Young. But not in my wildest imagination was I ready for the next individual to walk into the room: Dr. Martin Luther King Jr. When he walked into our meeting, for the first time in my life I was absolutely and completely tongue-tied. All I could do at that precise moment was think about my mother. My momma admired Dr. King so much, she could talk about him and tears would pool in the corners of her eyes. She felt like Dr. King was the first lieutenant to God, sent to this planet to heal the sins of this nation. At that moment, all I could think was, "Wow! I wish that my Mom could be a rock in my pocket or a bug on my lapel and just be here to take in this moment." I was in awe. I know I probably looked completely unnerved, but Dr. King had this way of putting the people around him at ease. He came out with such a warm manner—you could say an almost comedic style—and it relaxed all the young athletes who might have been starstruck in his presence.

If Dr. King had been born in another life and another skin, and didn't get involved in religion and the civil rights movement, he could have made a Brinks truck worth of money as a stand-up comic because he was so funny and charismatic, cracking jokes before the meeting, putting everyone in stitches and making us all comfortable. Then, with Dr. King present and accounted for, the meeting started in earnest. Dr. King made it clear from the beginning that he wasn't just there to lend moral support. He wanted to help us hammer out a plan and he made it clear that he would be a public supporter of the Olympic boycott. He also stated that while we had his public support, he wouldn't and couldn't be the lead man at the front of the march and in front of the cameras. He said that it would do the movement no favors. He wanted Harry Edwards to be the lead man, and said he would be very happy taking marching orders from Harry on this. Dr. King felt the boycott was a very worthy project and could prove to be a mighty platform to make clear the need to establish justice and equality for all men and women on this planet. He said that our strongest leverage was that an Olympic boycott could have a global reach. We could shock the world and we could do it by also adhering to the principles of nonviolence that he held so dear. We could bring attention to the problems of society, but we did not have to throw a rock or burn a building in order to do so.

This was Dr. King's methodology. He understood that militancy didn't mean violence. He understood that courage did not mean throwing punches. Sometimes it meant just the opposite. He also told us that if we wanted to go down and hold a demonstration during the Olympics in Mexico City, he would join us and bring the civil rights marches people knew from Selma and Montgomery right to the Mexican capital. I still remember him saying that he would get to work on that right after he saw through this garbage strike he was working on supporting in Memphis, Tennessee.

At the end of the meeting, I finally found my voice and was able to ask two questions of Dr. King. The first question I asked him, very respectfully, was why this idea of an Olympic boycott was attractive to him. He expressed to me that the concept and visual power of an Olympic boycott would be like a ripple in the water spreading throughout the world to let people know that the people of color of this earth were very disenchanted about their treatment and we could aspire to something better as a human race. He said that the visual power was in the void it would create: an

Olympics without black athletes. He said that the process would be like black soldiers stepping back from the military. "We're not saying 'burn it down,'" he said. "We're just merely saying we don't care to participate and see how you feel without us as a part of the show." I totally agreed. We weren't throwing any fire. We were just saying that we choose not to go. We felt like we had to step up because as I remember someone saying at the meeting, "If not us, who?" How do you become a "leader"? Well, it helps if you decide that you are going to lead.

My second question to Dr. King was something a lot of people in the room were wondering and it had nothing to do with anything that had to do with the Olympics. We wanted to know, "Why are you going back to Memphis when they are threatening your life?" Remember, Dr. King had been back and forth to Memphis where he was supporting a sanitation strike that had gotten so violent it became an article of faith that Dr. King had been marked for death. We all knew it. We knew that if someone had a clear shot at this great man, the trigger would be squeezed. He was addressing not just racism at home but also standing up against the war in Vietnam. He was just becoming too dangerous to too many people. At that moment, Dr. King made a very positive statement directly to me. He said, "John, I have to go back and stand for those that won't stand for themselves, and I have to go back for those that can't stand for themselves." The way he said it was very distinct and very precise. Once again, he said he had to "stand for those who won't stand for themselves, and stand for those who can't stand for themselves." Won't and can't: he had enough room in his heart for both.

When Dr. King said that, it made my life more certain. Maybe this is just the way I remember it more than forty years later, but that moment gave me a direction. Until then I was kind of a rebel without a cause, like Brando when they said, "What are you rebelling against?" and he replied,

"What have you got?" I never had any kind of a game plan or formula for what I was going to do in my life. I didn't have a compass. I would improvise and speak out against injustice as I saw it arise. But when Dr. King said those words to me, it was like he joined my mind and my heart and guided them toward one direction. This is when I became a heart and soul member of what we called the Olympic Project for Human Rights.

As we discussed that night, our demands as the OPHR had to go beyond just getting apartheid South Africa disinvited from the games. The fact that they had been readmitted in the first place spoke to how deep racism festered in the heart of the IOC. That was why one of the critical demands of OPHR was to remove Avery Brundage as head of the IOC. Now, I had never met Avery Brundage. I'd seen his rants on television, but that was about the extent of it. My impression was that Avery Brundage was very comfortable standing to the right of all things right wing. He came off like someone with money and power who couldn't or wouldn't hear what we were trying to say. I also felt like he was a puppet for other darker, even more reactionary, forces. He might've been the face of the IOC, but I think there were a lot of very powerful forces pushing him out front to be the tip of the spear. In other words, he had a lot of serious support behind the things he was saying. But as their figurehead, he hurt a great many people. He was the voice for apartheid South Africa and what was then known as Rhodesia. He was the voice saying that our concerns regarding having more African American coaches were irrelevant. He wasn't an honest broker for any nation of the global South. He had to go.

Tommy and Lee

By this time, I had also cemented my relationships with the gifted young men who would be seen as the leaders of the OPHR, Lee Evans and

Tommie Smith. I had met them before, but that was always in the heat of competition. I had gone west to San Jose State when we went to the nationals in 1965. To be honest with you, coming out of New York, I felt like they were country boys. I used to always bust their chops, saying to them, "Man, it's like you guys are still putting caps on your sneakers and wearing suspenders." But even then, as much as I called them "country," it was obvious that they had the highest abilities in the sport. I had nothing but respect and admiration for them and the talents that they brought to the track for each and every race.

Tommie in particular was someone I paid close attention to because we both ran the 200 meters and Tommie was the acknowledged number one runner of that race in the world. He was also the type of guy who would not race against the best competition, like myself, unless it was absolutely necessary. I understood why he had this approach to racing, but it still got under my skin. I respected Tommie and his abilities, but I also felt like our skills were commensurate. We should have been like Ali and Frazier in the lead-up to the 1968 Olympics, racing against each other every few months. But he avoided me like I had smallpox and we only ran head to head maybe five times over the course of my entire career.

I think the first time I ran against Tommie was in 1967 at the Los Angeles Coliseum. I was running in a relay with the great Jimmy Hines and some other guys from Houston. We called ourselves the Houston Striders and we formed a team to come out west to California, to run at the Coliseum. Tommie Smith was running the anchor leg in the mile relay, and so was I and I ran him down and we got kind of tangled up a little bit coming off that last turn. He kind of bumped me and got away from me, and I kind of ran back on him again, and he won the race, and I remember I was a little disturbed because I felt like we took second and it was okay, but then I found out later they weren't giving out second place prizes, which made it all the worse.

I think he was a little scared of me. I had already run 9.2 in the 100-yard dash and 20.2 in the 200. He and everyone had gotten word of this wild Mexican runner named Juan Carlos. There isn't a drop of Mexican blood in my body, but to this day, people call me Juan Carlos mistakenly. In California, with its large Mexican population, I had my own fan base waiting for me. The press asked me questions about my Mexican upbringing and I just never said a thing. I never said a word and let them think what they wanted to think. The *Los Angeles Times* even put my name out there as "Juan Carlos, the Mexican from Texas!" The *Times* also messed up my age and came up with a story of a twenty-seven-year-old Mexican freshman Juan Carlos running those times. But soon people knew I was just John Carlos from Harlem. When it came to Tommie, I had a chip on my shoulder. But when we started linking arms and making our case with the OPHR, that changed. Tommie stopped looking at me like a threat and I stopped looking at him like someone I was constantly trying to catch. From that time on, we were brothers in the struggle to build a boycott groundswell for the 1968 games.

In those early days of 1968, we really felt like we could make it happen. We had Dr. King on our side. We also happened to have the biggest, baddest athletes on earth on our side. We had the legendary Jackie Robinson, who broke baseball's color line in 1947, on our side. I have to say that I laugh when coaches and media talkers make the case that if an athlete is political, it somehow distracts from team concepts and winning. Four of the greatest winners in the history of sports were with us all the way: In the world of pro sports, we had Bill Russell and Jim Brown square in our corner. Bill Russell, the great Boston Celtics center, was in the midst of a run of winning eleven championships in thirteen years. He also was an outspoken opponent of racism and injustice in his adopted hometown of Boston. As for Jim Brown, he was pro football's all-time leading rusher and he led the Cleveland Browns to the 1964 NFL title. That's still the last title Cleveland has won in any sport. Russell and Brown supported us in the most helpful possible way. They were public. They showed up on all the talk shows and defended our efforts. But they also told us, "We will do whatever we can do to lend you support. But this is your ball of wax. Y'all are going to run this show. All we are going to do is be there to support you and do what you request of us." We asked them to go out and make the case for what we were doing and they did not disappoint. We also had Lew Alcindor, who of course would go on to change his name to Kareem Abdul Jabbar. Alcindor was in the middle of winning three straight NCAA titles at UCLA and he was militant. Hardly poisoning his team, that's for sure. Young Alcindor was public about how if there was a boycott, he would proudly adhere to it. Then there was the champion boxer Muhammad Ali. Restoring Ali's title was one of our central planks and it made me proud that he supported us and we supported him. Ali was young, gifted, and black. And he was proud of all three of those attributes. He was a gift from God to this society. And he protected the gift that God gave him. And then, once he converted to Islam and engaged with the Nation of Islam, he began to become educated. Ali, like me, had some learning disorders. But he was very sure of himself in terms of what knowledge he did have, and how he could use his knowledge and his fame for the greater good.

Ali represented black people. Ali represented his race. At the same time, there weren't a whole bunch of people jumping out there to support him, black or white. First of all, Ali didn't do anything to justify taking away his title. What they were doing to Ali, or attempting to do to Ali, was the same thing they were attempting to do to us in trying to taking our medals away. We were going to be punished for standing up for what we believed in. Ali was being punished for standing up for what he believed in. He said he was against the war in Vietnam. And he had a right to be against the war in Vietnam. Nobody really explained to the public why we should fight this war. When we were going through so much sinister stuff here in the United States, merely for the color of our skin, he made a very poignant statement when he said these people [the Vietnamese] have never done anything to us. And at the same time he was making that statement, I was making the statement that if the Vietnamese ever come across the Harlem River Bridge, I'll be the first one to pick up arms against them. But for us to go far away to a foreign land that most of us hadn't heard of, it's difficult for clear-thinking individuals to stand up and say, I'm going to go fight a war even though I know nothing about it. So, quite naturally, you want to support the individual that stands up for his own rights and for human rights generally.

I also liked Ali because I came from a military family. Two of my brothers were in the military. One was in the army and the other was in the air force. And I remember they used to tell me, "Johnny, it's your patriotic duty to go in the army, to join the war." And I said, for what? Those people ain't done nothing to me. My other brother stared at me and said, "If nothing else, Johnny, we get a chance to see the world." I laughed and put my arms around his shoulder and said, "My brother, there has to be a better way to see the world."

Challenges

This was the apex of our struggle, getting this kind of high-profile support. The low point of our situation was when we would have to argue with other young athletes about the need for them to support the boycott. They would look at us like they understood and agreed with us, but had no choice but to take a pass. It felt like they were saying to me, "Man, this is just the way life is. There's no changing anything. We can do it on the field and that needs to be good enough." It was almost like these guys were in quicksand, they could feel themselves sinking, and here we were trying to throw them a lifeline, but they were afraid to accept it.

We were taking our leadership from people like Bill Russell and Jim Brown, but the young runners resistant to the boycott had leaders and men of respect on their side as well. For instance all of us looked up to the great Olympic runner Ralph Boston. Ralph was the predominant competitive elder in our sport. He also was born in Mississippi. When Ralph was asked by the media about whether he felt the need to say something about racism in the United States during the Olympics, he said that he wouldn't know what to say because he had never experienced any kind of prejudice or racism in Mississippi when he was coming up as a youngster. This was a terrible untruth that he told to the media. He had certainly said otherwise when we were all together in the training room. So I was simply shocked to hear him say such a thing publicly, and I wasn't alone. There were several of us together at that time when we heard him make this statement, and our jaws just hit the floor. Ralph certainly wasn't alone in opposing the boycott or trying to put a smiley face on what it meant to be black in America at that time. The general assumption was that anyone who tried to mix sports and the politics of resistance would pay a terrible price. But by the end of the Olympics, Ralph was singing a very different tune. Like Harry Edwards wrote, by the time the Olympics were done, Ralph came back capital-B "Black."

But that story had yet to be written and Ralph was hardly alone in his misguidedness. In those early months of 1968, it was a sad situation to see my teammates, my comrades in athletic competition, pretending that they didn't know their history or how life was for themselves and their ancestors. Maybe they truly didn't know the blood and bondage that defined our history and our present. But I just find that impossible to believe. Far more likely, they were blinded by the glitter of a medal, or they just didn't care to see or understand what was happening right in front of their faces. Those of us who identified ourselves as part of the OPHR could only tell them that we couldn't make them accept the boycott. We weren't trying to coerce anyone to agree with us. We couldn't make them give up their Olympic dreams. No pressure. All we could do is put our ideas and demands on the table and hope that they could embrace them for themselves. But the desire for that medal had at this point become the great motivator in their lives. Actually, it was more than a motivator. It was their compass. It was like they'd been taken over by gold, silver, and bronze. They couldn't get around those medals and face the reality of life head-on.

Then two events occurred in April of 1968 that took the wind out of our sails. The first and most devastating was the assassination of Dr. King in Memphis. The loss of his presence, leadership, and moral authority was difficult enough. Seeing cities around the country burn as the man who epitomized nonviolence was gunned down tore us up. And most practically, we lost the vision of Dr. King joining us in Mexico City to protest outside the gates of the Olympic stadium. It was like we'd been kicked in the chest. The second event that took place later in the month was the rebanning of apartheid South Africa from the Olympics. Our pressure, at least on that front, had worked. But it also served to make a lot of our allies say, "Well, we accomplished that. So let's line up and go for the gold!"

There came a point after the events in April when people like Dr. Harry Edwards, Tommie Smith, Lee Evans, and I looked at each other and realized, "We don't really have the forces to pull this off." This happened at our last organizing meeting before we had to start either packing our bags for Mexico City or announce that we were staying home. We had to try and come to some sort of understanding of what we were going to do collectively and when we did a head count of who was in and who was out, it was obvious that there were too many people saying, "I am not willing or able or ready to sacrifice my opportunities in the Olympic Games for the sake of the boycott." The counterargument we made was "Your life is going to go on a lot longer after your Olympic medal moments and what standard of living do you expect to have? We have a chance to make a difference right here, right now." We were very lonely at this point in standing for the boycott. It's funny because today, you see many individuals trying to rewrite that history and make it seem like back then they were standing with us every step of the way. But what they were saying in reality was, "I understand what you are coming for, I just don't want to hear it, not when there is a medal to be won." I think of Charlie Green, Ralph Boston, Bob Beamon. Before the games, all these guys wanted the taste of Olympic glory more than they wanted a life as a three-dimensional man. They wanted to be princes of their sport even if it meant being a pauper when the uniform came off.

At the time, I thought their heads were in the past and Harry, Tommy, Lee, and I were the voices of the future. But in many ways, these guys who opposed the boycott and saw their individual achievement above all else tragically had a better handle on where the world was going. Getting yours, the hell with everybody else, forgetting about your sisters and brothers: this has defined our modern era, and it defined these hardheaded teammates of ours. I remember getting heated, saying, "Man, what we are talking about ain't sports. It's life! Who cares if you go through life without a medal? So what? Everyone can't be an Olympic champion, but by staying home you could represent so many individuals who would never come close to the Olympic Games. By going, you are representing yourself and you are selling an image of this country to the world that just ain't the truth. By boycotting, you are with everyone."

But we couldn't pull it off. After Dr. King was murdered and the IOC folded on South Africa, the other athletes just weren't hearing what we were trying to say. People were carrying themselves differently. You could see it in their faces, their shoulders, and their attitudes. They were done with this boycott talk.

Now it was down to just a few of us and the question was right there on the table for all the OPHR diehards: were we all actually going to go to the Olympic Games or would we do an entirely symbolic, ineffective boycott made up of people you could count on one hand? We had taken so much heat in the media for the boycott call, and heat from the coaches, from the track federations, from the IOC, and we were ready to stand up to all of it. But we weren't prepared to shovel sand in the ocean. We weren't prepared to look weak. We had no choice but to fold our tent. At this time, we had no thoughts of symbolic protest at the games themselves. We were dissatisfied that our teammates didn't have heart enough to stand with us. I was ticked off, and Harry and Tommy and Lee were just disenchanted.

After we decided to shut it down, the biggest thing I had to decipher in my mind and heart was whether I would just stay at home anyway. I was just so angry at everybody and everything, I wasn't sure if I'd have the stomach for any of it. I remember I had a discussion with Kareem. Kareem was saying that he still didn't want to go. I said to him, "Man, let me tell you something, you're going to be the heart of the NBA. You will be getting paid to play basketball for years to come whether you go or not. If you choose not to go and say you want to stay home to pursue your studies, who is going to argue with you?" That's exactly what he did.

I wanted to stay home as well, but after much deliberation, I decided that I simply couldn't. I felt if I stayed home that someone would win a medal and get on the podium—and be standing where I was meant to stand. I just felt they were not going to represent what I wanted and needed to be represented at that medal moment. It was imperative that I make the team now. It was imperative to me that I win a medal because if I wasn't staying home, I wanted to be in Mexico City to express my feelings. I wasn't sure what I was going to do, but something had to be done, and I was going to do it.

Right: That's little me, with my cousin Mary, who never let me leave the house with her if I wasn't dressed and bundled.

Left: We didn't take many photos growing up. There is one of me as a little boy.

Below: That's Kim. She is a teenager in this picture. We were both teenagers when we married.

The man in the middle is my blood uncle . . . he was a great man. I include this just to show that as hung up as we are on color in this country, we are more connected and similar than we realize.

Left, above: Kim and me with Jerry and Ethel Williams on the field of the San Jose State Track.

Left, below: Jerry Williams beat both Tommie Smith and me in this 100-meter race at San Jose State in early 1968.

Below: At the 1968 AAU championships.

Jeff Kroot

Above, right: Tommie and me in a mellow stretch before a race. Relaxation is key before you line up to run. Above, left: Tommie and me talking strategy before a race.

Running a full spring in black shades was a sign of the times. Along with black socks, they indicated that you were down for the struggle on the track and off.

Above: Taking the baton at San Jose State. Per usual, I would get it with a lead already in place.

Left: These were the buttons worn by supporters and participants in the Olympic Project for Human Rights. Every once in a while one resurfaces. I'll never forget the Harvard Olympic Crew Team bringing a whole stack to the '68 games.

Right: This is the poster that was meant to show the internationalism and unity OPHR was trying to represent. This wasn't just about Black America. It was about Africa. It was about standing with the struggles in apartheid nations fighting for their freedom.

Peter Norman, Tommie Smith, and me on the Olympic podium during our medal stand.

Tommie (right) and me contemplating our futures after the medal stand moment put us on newspapers across the globe.

Tommie in front, Kim and me behind him as we leave Mexico City in 1968 after our explusion.

Here is my friend Bob Beamon who shocked the world by jumping 29 feet and 2.5 inches at the 1968 games. He later wore black socks on the medal stand to protest our expulsion.

We were all friends, teammates, and competitors. Standing L–R: Larry Questad, Lennox Miller, Kirk Clayton, Jimmie Hines; kneeling L–R: Ernie Provost, Mel Pender, Charlie Greene. This was taken at the "Night of Speed" at the 1968 AAU Track and Field Championships 100 meters.

1969 was my best year as a runner. Here I am for Speed City, San Jose State, running 100 yards in nine seconds flat.

Courtesy of San Jose State University

Left: Tommie Smith and me at the unveiling of our statue at San Jose State.

Below: 2008 Penn Relays, speaking with the young members of the North Carolina Central Track Team.

Derek Tolliver

Derek Tolliver

Derek Tolliver

Above: Me with my son, a twenty-year member of the US Army and Marine Corps, Malik Carlos.

Special thanks to Derek L. Toliver for his indispensable help compiling these photos.

Five

■   ■   ■   ■

The Medal Stand

The question people always ask is about premeditation—did I go to Mexico City knowing I was going to raise my fist on the medal stand? Did Tommie know? Did Harry Edwards or Lee Evans know? The answer is that no one on the planet, including us, had any sense going into those games that we were going to make any kind of political statement that would both get us in a world of trouble and stand the test of time. But in the last meeting we had before we all left for Mexico City, when we knew the boycott had fallen through and we were stewing in our juices, the collective decision was that we would go to the games and each person would do their own thing. Whatever they felt was the right thing to do would get done, and we'd have each other's back. That was the last word, and that was the thought left simmering inside our heads. But first, for all of us, there was the little matter of making the team.

I had no reservations whatsoever that I would make the team. As the saying went, "speed don't lie." I was in the best shape of my life and I had won seventeen of the last eighteen races I entered. Tommie and Lee were also at the top of their game. Tommie and I would be competing against each other in the 200 meters and Lee would run in the 400. All of us, in the thin Mexico City air at that elevation, were acknowledged threats to rewrite the record books.

The question was really what would we do when—not if—we made it to the medal stand. We had stature, and this made us dangerous. The United States Olympic Committee feared what we would do, and I heard later that they were trying to figure out how to weed us out. The problem for them, however, was that if the United States didn't get the expected number of medals and records, people in the USOC would lose their jobs. They needed us, they hated us, and they feared us all at the same time.

There were two trials for the team: the first one was in Los Angeles at the Coliseum, and then the second and final trial was in Tahoe. But they said that whoever made the team at the first trials was on the team. They took Tommie and put him in lane eight, the outside lane, to make it as hard on him as humanly possible. I had a bad leg at the time, so bad I couldn't run the 100 meters as I dreamed, so I concentrated on the 200 meters with Tommie. If Tommie's lane eight was difficult enough because of the wide turn, they did me one worse and put me in lane one, which is the lane in the 200 meters with absolutely the sharpest turn you can imagine. But fortunately, by the grace of God, we both qualified to move up and guess what? We made the team and there was nothing they could do about it.

Then in Tahoe, my leg had healed again, and I took it a step further, but once again the murky world of politics outside my control was swirling against me. I ran the 200 meters in 19.7 seconds, by a country mile, a new world record. Then the IAAF (International Association of Athletics Federation) stepped in and nullified the record. Why? Because I was wearing "brush spike" sneakers, newly produced by Puma. At the time, Adidas was waving a whole lot of money in front of the IAAF. Also, I was someone they were constantly trying in vain to make sit down and shut up. Not only did I refuse to shut my mouth, but anything that was broadcasting Puma was frowned upon as well. The great irony in all this is that these kind of brush spikes, or variations of spiked track shoes are the norm today, as runners like Usain Bolt are doing this distance in 19.19 seconds.

I was feeling strong. I knew they would try to knock me down, but it didn't matter as long as I crossed that finish line first. I was ready to do it again in the 100 meters and I was knocking it out in the 100, setting records in the trials. But officials stepped in and said that I wasn't allowed at the starting line because I hadn't run it in Los Angeles, even though I was hurt there and running the best 100 times in the world. It was unbelievable. At the time, the United States dominated the 100 meters and sure enough, we did win the gold, thanks to Jimmy Hines, but I knew that my exclusion was all political. To this day I shake my head because their big critique of us was that we were mixing politics and sports, which is supposed to be a politics-free zone, and here they were, mixing politics and sports, not letting me try out for the race because of my political beliefs. They were disappointed that I was still speaking out with conviction even after deciding to go to Mexico City. When they wouldn't let me race, I blew up like a volcano. I jumped up and down. I was furious. I wanted to go to the USOC headquarters and say, "You have forty-eight hours to make this right!"

I heard later that at one of the reunions of that team, which I did not attend, the assistant coach, the legendary Stan Wright, stepped up to the plate and said to people, "Everything that John said was the truth. He was kept out of the 100 meters for political reasons." I don't have any misgivings about the fact that Jimmy Hines was our 100-meter man and he won the gold. It wasn't anything that Jimmy did. It was what Avery Brundage and the Olympic officials did in keeping me from running that race. In some ways though, I've had the revenge of history on my side because I saw a quote from Jimmy Hines saying, "Everywhere I go, I say I was in the '68 Olympics. All anybody can ask me about is, 'Oh, were you one of the guys on the podium?'" Now, I'm sorry Jimmy Hines and others have to deal with that, but that's something they have to live with, because they ran from the moment. We all could've been the guy on the podium raising his fist or the guy stepping away from the podium. There is sweetness in the spirit of God. The fact is that God made them realize that they should have stood with us by having to answer the question of whether they were one of those guys on the podium.

It's satisfying because at the time, a lot of the runners thought we were pure poison. When we were in the airport in Washington, DC, heading out to Mexico City, Bob Beamon said to me, "Man, you screwed up your life. When these Olympics are over, you ain't never going nowhere." I was hurt because they were sitting there at four o'clock in the morning telling me this in the airport. I remember telling him, "Let me ask you something: Did you ever see a hummingbird or a helicopter that just hovers and stays in a state of limbo? That's what I'm doing. I'm not down and out, man. I'm just waiting to make the right move. I'm just praying, because when I go up again and I will be going up again right to the top, I will treat you better than you're treating me right now."

But I had more on my mind then than sniping and backbiting. We were on our way to Mexico City and we knew that a serious social crisis was going to be greeting us when we got off the plane. In that first week of October 1968, just a few short days before the opening of the games, there was a river of young blood in the Mexican streets. Hundreds of students from the state university were massacred by the state military in Mexico City's Tlatelolco Square. Apparently the students had been protesting nonviolently all year and the confrontations with the police had been mild. But now the Olympics were coming up and students had started using slogans incorporating the Olympics, asking how their country could have money for the games while people went hungry. Well, someone snapped somewhere, because on government orders, the troops and their military leaders stopped such talk in as extreme a way as possible, cornering the students in the public square and butchering them like hogs, all in the name of making Mexico City "presentable" for an international audience. The protesting students, with all their idealism, were collateral damage. After more than forty years, the families of these young people still haven't had anything like real justice for these murders.

To the great shame of the Olympic movement, all that bloodshed and death was never mentioned once during the games nor has it ever been mentioned in any Olympic-sanctioned event ever since. I believe that they, not Tommie and me, are the true Olympic martyrs, and they must never be forgotten. We discussed it on the plane going down there because for us, this was more than just talk. They were in the original drafts for our statement in Mexico City.

After Dr. King died and we decided to forgo the boycott, our next plan was to have Harry Edwards, Tommie Smith, Lee Evans, and myself go to Mexico City early before the team got there, and hook up with the Mexican students who had been protesting and occupying the campus for most of that year. We wanted to convene with them for some sort of cross-border solidarity action and create a sense of common cause. They were upset about the way the Olympics were being used to create a false vision for a global audience about the realities of Mexico. We were upset about the way the Olympics were being used to create a false vision of what it meant to be black in America. It was a natural connection. We later found out that both governments were very aware that this could be a plan of action. We don't know if they were killed to keep from hooking up with us. We don't know if we could have ended up in that pile of bodies. This might sound over the top, but back then with Dr. King being killed, Bobby Kennedy being killed, the students being killed, nothing seemed that far-fetched.

After the massacre, Harry decided that there was no point in coming with us to Mexico City. He wasn't an athlete anymore and had no official standing on the team. He could have gone down anyway as an act of unity, but he expressed publicly to the press that he was concerned about credible threats on his life that would be carried out if he made the trip. At the time, being young, I was extremely upset with him. Yes, he had threats on his life, but Tommie, Lee, and I had an unholy mountain of death threats on our shoulders as well. People were sending us bullets in the mail, for goodness' sake. I felt like his life was no more important and no less important than ours. As runners, we didn't even have the time to look over our shoulders to see if someone might have a scope on us. We still had a job to do. This was a time before metal detectors at the stadium so we knew we'd just be out there on the track defenseless. We had to race. So, I thought it was a poor move on his part to say he wasn't going to go to the games because of death threats. But with the benefit of age, I see now that I didn't know what was in Harry's head or the degree of threat he was under or how that affected his loved ones. I know Harry was down with us from jump, and I now understand the need to save my arrows for those who deserve them.

But for us, in Mexico City, we never felt safe. Whether we were in Olympic Village, or meeting with the team, or just concentrating on the race ahead: it was like every day you got out of bed, wondering if your head would make it back to hit the pillow that night. All you could say was, "I'm in the hands of God. I can't be worried if somebody's trying to hurt me. All I can do is just think about what I have to do." I didn't want to be a prisoner of fear so I focused on preparing myself, and getting a feel for the people of the country, keeping my eyes and my ears open. Fortunately for me, Kim was there with me to soothe my nerves. Also fortunately for me, we were able to get out of Olympic Village and stay at a much safer, more remote location. Kim and I stayed with Bob Beamon and his lady friend at a villa that had been rented by one of the old sponsors from my Pioneer Club days, a gentleman by the name of Mel Zahn. It gave Kim and me some sane surroundings where we could think and relax.

At this point, Tommie and I hadn't said even one word to each other about what we were going to do if we both made it to the medal podium. That changed once we saw each other on the track. Tommie and I came together in an early heat called the quarter-semi and I told Tommie I was still stewing about the fact that the boycott went up in smoke and I wanted to make some sort of statement. Tommie's head was in exactly the same place. He knew that this was our time to make our stand. But at the same time, for Tommie it was different. Maybe it was because he was the number one in the world and the acknowledged favorite coming in. Or perhaps it was because of all of us he had taken the most body blows from the press for even talking about a boycott. For two years Tommie had taken these blows and I know now that we were racing he wanted to shove it back in everyone's face. But whatever drove Tommie, I could tell that for him, the only acceptable ending was to make his political statement from the gold medal perch and the gold medal perch alone.

As for me, I didn't care a lick if I won the gold, silver, or bronze. I wasn't there for the race. I was there for the after-race. I made it clear to Tommie that we would both be on that medal stand. Tommie nodded his head with a dead-serious look on his face and then we started talking about the symbols we would use. We had no guide, no blueprint. No one had ever turned the medal stand into a festival of visual symbols to express our feelings. We decided that we would wear black gloves to represent strength and unity. We would have beads hanging from our neck, which would represent the history of lynching. We wouldn't wear shoes to symbolize the poverty that still plagued so much of black America. On the medal stand, all we would wear on our feet would be black socks.

Once we decided on the "symbology," we had to figure out how to get our hands on the symbols. Fortunately, my wife Kim had the beads and was down with our plan all the way. Tommie's wife at the time had the black gloves. It's an interesting detail of history that she had only brought the gloves to Mexico City because Tommie had told her that if he medaled and was in a position in which he had to shake Avery Brundage's hand, he didn't want to have to touch the old man's skin. Of course we had our own black socks, which were the style at the time.

Once we had our symbols in order, there was not a shred of doubt that this was something that had to be done. I was truly ashamed of my country. I understood it perfectly when Michelle Obama supposedly "misspoke" in the 2008 campaign and said that she'd never been proud of her country before that campaign. I think anyone who ever had to be raised in this skin in this country knew what she was talking about. I say that because I remember that moment when I was locked in on the medal stand protest and I knew in my gut that it wasn't just about 1968. It wasn't just about Vietnam, Dr. King's assassination, the murders of the Mexican students, or this media tag about some Age of Aquarius "Revolt of the Black Athlete." It was about everything that led up to 1968. It was about the stories my father told me about fighting in the First World War. It was about the terrible things he was asked to do for a freedom he was denied when he returned home.

It was about him being told where he could live, where his kids could go to school, and how low the ceiling would be on his very life. I thought about how long ago the First World War seemed to me. It felt, on the one hand, like a time and place beyond my understanding. But on the other hand, I thought about how similar things were in 1968 compared to those long ago days. I thought about a world where I was encouraged to run but not to speak.

Then I thought about Jesse Owens. I thought about those four golds he won in Berlin representing the United States, each medal a smack to the side of Hitler's face. I thought about how for a moment that made Jesse a hero, but then when he came home, he was racing horses for money. I thought about how Jesse was now so turned around he didn't support our efforts to speak out about our condition.

Then I thought about a man who did speak out on our behalf, Mr. Jackie Robinson. I thought about what he endured with such dignity on the field, but it was twenty years later and we were still catching hell. I thought about something Jackie was saying a lot in speeches those days: "It doesn't matter that I made it in sports. More important is the condition of the masses of people." That made me think about education in our community, how it was something special, even jaw-dropping, to have a member of your family make it to a top university in the United States, especially if they did it without the help of a ball or a fast time in the 100 meters.

I thought about how humiliating and difficult it was for a black man to get a decent job to support his family. At the same time, while education was hard to find, the pusher man wasn't. I thought about the way drugs were as easy to find as a bottle of soda pop in any ghetto in America. I thought about Harlem when I was growing up and how people overnight would become junkies, shells of people, zombies before my young eyes. I thought about all the greatness that black people had brought to the table for America, how we built this country from the sweat of our brows and arches of our backs, and then, in turn, we were always second-class citizens. We could go out and win medals. We could go out and win wars. We could break all the world records, and we could be heroes as long as we stayed in between the lines. But once we got off the field, we were just regular old nothings. I was very saddened by that, and felt that somebody needed to get up and make a statement and to the planet Earth and say, "Hey, world, the United States is not like you might think it is for blacks and other people of color. Just because we have 'USA' on our chest does not mean everything is peachy keen and we are living large." I remember when we started to make noise about the boycott, a rising snarl started to rise from people who said, "You should be happy that we allowed you to go represent America in the Olympic Games." I would always think to myself, "Happy? Happy to not be able to feed our families? Happy to live in ghettoes with more drugs than hope? Happy to graduate as a people from slavery to athletics and second-class citizenship? Walk in my shoes and see if you smile."

The person who most staggered Lee, Tommie, me and honestly just about everyone else on the US track squad was the legend himself, Jesse Owens. I had an opportunity to meet Jesse in Mexico City and make no mistake: he was there to try and stop us from doing anything political on the track. He was there to make sure that no politics damaged the

"Olympic movement." I truly had more charity in my heart for Jesse than most. I knew he was old school. I knew, from my experience at East Texas, that this struggle was generational more than it was racial and that Jesse was from another generation.

But I could see why it shocked my teammates to see Jesse coming out so strongly against us. The IOC, led by Avery Brundage, had scorned and shunned Jesse for decades for the crime of being a black superstar. They didn't even let Jesse back in the stadiums or put him in front of a microphone until we started talking smack about our boycott in 1966. That's thirty years later. Then the IOC took Jesse, put a suit on him, stuffed some money in his pocket, and told him, "We want you to be the voice of the good black American." The next thing you knew, Jesse was in our locker room saying to us, "Hey, the greatest thing is to represent the United States in the Olympic Games."

Years after we did what we did, he and I had a chance to talk, before he died. After putting our heads together for a while, Jess said, "John, I realized after a time that we were shooting for the same thing. We wanted peace, love, and harmony amongst all the races. You were going about it your way and I was going about it my way. And I feel as though you made more headway 'going strong' than I ever did with mine."

But it's now a sad part of his legacy that Brundage sent him into the locker room to try and calm us down and prevent us from making any kind of statement. He came into the locker room and said, "If you wear those black socks, you're not going to be able to race as fast," and people just looked at him like, "You don't even understand why we are wearing these socks."

After Tommie and I did our thing, Jesse accosted us gruffly and said, "Why are you using those black gloves, those false props?" He used the words "false props." And I said, "What are you talking about false props?" And he said, "Those black gloves." And I said to him right away, "Well, Mr. Owens, these gloves are to let you know that we are representing black people before we represent anyone, anything, any symbol, any flag, or any nation. This is Technicolor, sir. We want to be very clear about who we are representing. That's what these black gloves are all about."

He was old school all right. I know that some of the guys saved a special kind of hostility for him. Lee Evans wasn't the only person calling him an Uncle Tom. I know this hurt Jesse terribly because he felt like he was a black man too. To be scorned by your own in the sport that you love so much, I'm sure that it was like a blade in his heart. But he had no real sway over us. His efforts to move us politically were in a different language from what the rest of us were talking. It sounded like there wasn't any time when Jesse tried to say anything other than what they handed him on a script. He would be in the locker room haranguing us to find our patriotic souls and give up the thought of making any kind of statement. The one time I became short with him, I looked Jesse up and down and said, "Mr. Owens, you know if you had stood up in 1936 a little more, we wouldn't have to in 1968."

It was a sad thing for him to be in that predicament because from those 1968 games, Jesse became very scarred, and the scar tissue had two layers: one from how he thought that he was doing the right thing by serving the Olympic committee and another because he felt like black people believed he wasn't worth the time of day since he staked out a position as the man trying to stop us from doing what we did.

Years later when we spoke, he said to me, "Maybe the truest thing is that if I had done more in 1936, we wouldn't have needed a 1968." I feel for Jesse Owens. I truly do. Jackie Robinson was more the person we looked to. Jackie, as I mentioned, supported the boycott. Jackie was a veteran and to have him say that we were on the right side of history was a powerful thing to carry with us. He had his finger on the social pulse and knew exactly what was going on. Earlier that year, he had quit the Republican Party and Richard Nixon's campaign because of the feel of racism on the march in that political party at that particular time. He was public about that, so his skin was plenty thick enough to step out and support our boycott with no reservations whatsoever. When you consider the series of humiliations that he had to go through for being an athlete, it was humbling that he felt we were part of his historical arc. Jackie had to go to war with his own teammates to even get a chance. And then of course, he also had to be great, and he was. None of us in 1968 ever had to do that. We may have had teammates who disagreed with our politics, but no one ever got in our faces with the kind of vitriolic confrontations that Jackie had to deal with. That's critical, because the press or the fans could be as nasty as they wanted to be, but a team is supposed to be a citadel of support. Jackie didn't even have that.

Jackie also taught us that it wasn't about his time, and it wasn't about our time. It was about times to come. The least important thing was whether we would medal. The most important thing was that we were heard. But here was where I differed with Jackie slightly. I knew that all this would be just talk and forgotten the next day unless we medaled in the 200 meters and had the space to make our stand.

Before the race started, I made up my mind that I wasn't going to test Tommie for that gold medal. I wanted Tommie to win the gold. I told this to our coach, Bud Winters. Coach told me, "You do what you need to do." I looked over and smiled and said, "You know I'm-a do it. You know I'm-a do it." It was time to stop the talk and get ready for the big race.

At the same time, we had another challenge before us. In that quarter-semi, Tommie hurt himself, pulling his groin muscle. Now, if a man hurts his groin muscle, I don't care how much tranquilizer or Novocain they shoot into your body—they can numb you to the point of paralysis and you're still not going to be able to run your best. But Tommie gritted his teeth and braved himself through it. It gave me an indication of what kind of courage and competitive fire burned within this man. It also let me know just how much the race and the gold meant to Tommie.

Finally it was time for the finals. It was time to forget the political atmosphere and just focus on the next twenty seconds of our lives. There were at least fifty thousand people in attendance, including a huge American contingent. Everyone was glued to watching our event because of the controversy we evoked and the records we could break. When the race popped off, we were all rolling. I have to say, I was flying, man. When that gun went off, I was gone. When I came up to the turn, I had everybody beat by at least six meters, maybe seven meters. Tommie then shook off his groin problems and had his "Tommie Legs" pumping. Before his "Tommie Legs" kicked it, I kept looking over my left shoulder to see where the hell Tommie was. I was screaming in my brain, "Come on Tommie! Stop bullshitting and come on!" I had to make sure he got his kick in and would be there with me. You can see as we approach the finish line, I turn one last time over my left shoulder, to see where Tommie is so I'm sure we're both on point for the medal stand. Now if you notice, I don't look over my right shoulder once in the entire race except at that very micro-fraction of a second when we cross the finish line. At that last moment, I saw a white blur and said to myself, "Oh shit. It's Peter Norman."

Tommie set a world record that day that held almost twenty years, running 200 meters in 19.87 seconds. Peter and I both ran 20 flat but I knew as soon as we crossed the tape that he beat me by a whisker. Frankly, I thought if a white man could run a 200 meter in 20 flat, he deserved to win silver. I was especially happy about the fact that if it had to be anyone, it was Peter.

Peter Norman was an Australian sprinter, the best one that country has ever produced by far. He also was sympathetic to the boycott cause and to the cause of peace and freedom for all people. Peter was a man of heart and conscience. But he was also one hell of an athlete. I liked his attitude and his moxie. He was a white boy from Australia and he would walk right up to us in the trials and say, "You ain't shit." I would say right back, "You ain't shit, and I'm going to spank your ass tomorrow," and that kind of thing, back and forth. After a while, it evolved to the point where we were saying it with a wink and a smile. The best part was that he talked smack right back at me on the track, and then showed love for our political cause off the track.

We had a shared respect and bonded from that point on. As the rounds and the trials went on, it was obvious that the three of us were the class of the 200-meter group. We got to talking a lot about politics, the failed boycott, and the need to make some kind of stand, but not being sure exactly what that would be. Before the 200-meter finals, the three of us were in the tunnel and we hipped Peter to what we were going to try and do after the race. I remember I asked him, "We are the Olympic Project for Human Rights. Do you believe in human rights?" And he told me right there in that tunnel about how his mother and father worked for the Salvation Army all his life, and he said, "Of course, I believe in human rights." I said, "If you make it to the podium with us, would you like to wear the Olympic Project for Human Rights button?" Without saying a word, he started reaching for mine like a kid in a candy store. I just about smacked his hand. "You can't have this one, but we'll get you one," I told him. The Harvard crew team journeyed to Mexico with a big bag of buttons and slipped one to Peter before the race. Peter's gone now. He passed away far too young in 2006. But I don't think too many days go by during the course of the week that I don't think about him. Peter had a beautiful soul and he endured hell when he went home to Australia after the Olympics. The press treated him terribly: he was the white man who stood with those two aboriginal devils, John Carlos and Tommie Smith. I have always said, Tommie and I had each other, but Peter was by himself. After the 1968 games, when we came back home to the States, one day the press would kick my ass, then take a break and kick Tommie's. But in Australia, they were on Peter twenty-four, seven. You couldn't even say that Peter disrespected his flag or his country. He merely wore a button supporting human rights and said, "I believe in supporting humanity in every way that we can to make this a better world." He was shut out of the Australian track and field world and even though he was the most accomplished sprinter in that country's history, when Sydney hosted the Olympics in 2000, there was not even a ceremonial role to be found for one Peter Norman. But I will say this: in all the years that went by, I never heard Peter complain once publicly. He was a man without ego. But as I learned in that race, he was also one hell of an athlete.

If you studied Peter Norman, you knew that in every race he ran, the last 20 meters were the most explosive. That's when I finally looked over and said, "Oh shit, Peter Norman. I forgot about him." If you look at the tape, you can see that at the end I'm striding in the race, not running. You look at it and after 60 or 70 meters, you see me striding. When I saw Peter there, I was toast. Once you break from a sprint to a stride, it's near impossible, with 10 meters to go, to go back into a full sprint. All I could do was go forward and lean into the tape. But as you can see on my face, I was elated. I was elated that he could run 20 flat. I was elated that I had run 20 flat doing the shit that I did. And then looking at Tommie with his arms stretched and joy creased into his face, I felt in my gut that it came out the way it was supposed to come out.

That race was brotherhood in motion. Tommie Smith is my brother. We are bonded in a way that no two other people on earth are bonded. We've had our differences and problems over the years, but when the fortieth anniversary of the 1968 games rolled through in 2008, we made a series of public appearances together, talked a great deal with each other, and brought our lives back into realignment. It was a reminder to both of us that, in the grand scheme of things, the race was just the preamble. We had the main event waiting for us on the medal stand.

We've Been Trained to Listen to the Gun

Tommie had his gold, I had my bronze, and we both had a place on that podium, just like we always wanted. Just like we saw it. We walked to the medal stand—our gloves were on, our beads were on, our shoes were off, and through the elation, the rapturous cheers from the crowd, and the titanic surge of adrenaline from the race, a new feeling took over my body. I felt the focus I used to feel when I did my time in the Golden Gloves. I was thinking, "The race is over. Time for the main event. Let's get it on!" Tommie was in a different place. He was so jacked about setting a world record and hearing all the cheers that he broke out in this big smile and pumped both hands in the air, even though one of them had a black glove on it already! I was worried he couldn't bring it back to the kind of serene focus we had aspired to, but then as we climbed up on the stand, my mind went far away from what Tommie was doing. I started reflecting on my dad, the stories he told me about what he endured in the armed forces. I thought about Harlem and the way the integrated community of my youth became all black, with the money and the opportunity moving away with the white residents. I reflected on the fact that my dad told me with pain in his eyes that I wasn't going to be able to make it to the Olympics in swimming, not because of my abilities, but because of the color of my skin. I pondered what Malcolm always said about being true to yourself even when it hurts. I thought about Dr. King's words about why he had to go back to Memphis even though his life was in jeopardy—because he felt a calling to stand for those people who "couldn't or wouldn't stand for themselves." And then finally I thought about my family, my refuge, Kim and Kimme, and I thought, "Damn. When this thing is done, it can't be taken back."

I know that sounds like a lot of thoughts for just a few moments standing on a podium before the start of the national anthem, but honestly this was all zigzagging through my brain like lightning bolts. It was like flashes of light dancing in my mind amidst raindrops. Before the anthem started to play, I purposefully took a moment to reflect on the artifacts we had chosen. I looked at my feet in my high socks and thought about all the black poverty I'd seen from Harlem to East Texas. I fingered my beads and thought about the pictures I'd seen of the "strange fruit" swinging from the poplar trees of the South. When we were up there, I made the personal decision to keep my jacket open, which was a major breech of Olympic etiquette, to remember all the working-class people—black and white—in Harlem who had to struggle and work with their hands all day. I thought about the fact that I covered up the "USA" on my chest with a black T-shirt to reflect the shame I felt that my country was traveling at a snail's pace toward something that should be obvious to all people of good will. Then the anthem started and we raised our fists into the air. If you look at the pictures, Tommie's fist and back are so straight it looks like he was drawn up with a protractor. My arm is slightly bent. That was because I wanted to make sure in case someone rushed us, I could throw down a hammer punch to protect us. We had just received so many threats leading up to that point that I refused to be defenseless at the moment of truth.

As the anthem began and the crowd saw us raise our fists, the stadium became eerily quiet. For a few seconds, you honestly could have heard a frog piss on cotton. There's something awful about hearing fifty thousand people go silent, like being in the eye of a hurricane. Then, as the national anthem played in full force, the calm before the storm ended and the boos started coming down. The people who weren't booing were screaming the national anthem. Seriously. It didn't sound like the people from the United States were singing it. It sounded like they were screaming it. It was like they were saying, "Oh, you anti-American sons of bitches. We're going to shove this shit down your throat!" They screamed it to the point where it seemed less a national anthem than a barbaric call to arms. I thought about what Tommie and I had already said to each other: "If anybody has a high-power rifle and they hit the trigger, just remember that we've been trained to listen to the gun. So, just focus and hit the deck."

Then, when the anthem had mercifully ended, we started walking back to the tunnel. That's when the boos started to come in earnest. The shock was gone and it was officially getting ugly. People were throwing things at us from the stands, and I heard some people yell, "Niggers need to go back to Africa!" Someone else yelled ,"I can't believe this is how you niggers treat us after we let you run in our games."

Then as we were walking off the field, Tommie made me very proud. As the shit and slurs were falling all around us, he looked as mad as I've

ever seen a Southern boy look and he threw his fist up sky-high in the face
of these boos. I yelled out, "Right on!" I was ready to get off that track,
proud that we'd said our piece. But I had no idea the moment on the
medal stand would be frozen for all time. I had no idea what we'd face. I
didn't know or appreciate at that precise moment, that the entire trajectory
of our young lives had just irrevocably changed.

Fallout

We didn't know what the fallout would be. We had no idea. But I got a
glimpse on the athletes' bus after our medal stand moment. The bus was
to take us back to Olympic Village. I was going to talk with some teammates
there and then go out to the villa and figure out with Kim what we were
going to do and how long we were going to stay in Mexico City. But there
was a guy on the bus with his wife and his two daughters. I don't even begin
to know how he got on the bus. He must have been connected in some
way with the IOC. But the guy, in front of his whole family, on a crowded
bus, just started ribbing me hard: "Oh, there's the guy who spit on my flag,"
he said. "You must be some kind of communist." I'm listening to the dude
and we got to the point where I had enough, and I said, 'Hey, man, let me
tell you something. First of all, you're on our bus. You're taking our seats.
You're not an athlete. Your family members aren't athletes. And you're
steady running your mouth." His wife is trying to tell her husband to be
quiet, but he had himself worked into a frothing lather. He kept saying,
"You must be a communist, you must be a communist." I didn't even know
what a communist was. The crazy part was that I was much bigger than
this man. I was surrounded by my teammates—my people—and still this
joker felt confident enough to take shots at me without censor or shame. I
knew from that moment on that Tommie and I would have conflicts and

confrontations like that probably for the rest of our lives. What I didn't know then was just how they would reach and affect my family.

When we made it back to Olympic Village, there were athletes, to my shock, who were incredibly supportive. Even some who strongly opposed any thought of a boycott had our backs. They didn't throw us under the bus and it gave me a great feeling of hope. One of our teammates, Vincent Matthews, put up a sign that read, "We support Smith and Carlos."

Maybe these other athletes didn't do demonstrations like we did, and maybe they didn't boycott, but they fully felt and understood why it was necessary for us to do what we did. Black, white, male, female, no matter the country, you can't find one example of anyone on that team throwing us under the bus. The team mentality was just too tight. But while they never walked away from us, very few walked closely to us either. There were of course exceptions. The one closest to my heart was the anchor of the women's gold-medal-winning 4x100 team, Wyomia Tyus. Wyomia said after their victory, "I'd like to say that we dedicate our relay win to John Carlos and Tommie Smith." The Harvard crew team also stood up for us with a great statement. "We—as individuals—have been concerned about the place of the black man in American society in their struggle for equal rights," read the statement. "As members of the US Olympic team, each of us has come to feel a moral commitment to support our black teammates in their efforts to dramatize the injustices and inequities which permeate out society," it continued. They put that together right in the aftermath, and it meant a great deal to Tommie and me. But most of the athletes acted as if they stood close to us, they would get shit on their suits. As the saying goes, "They done shot us up with the shit gun."

Then just as we were assessing the situation and figuring out where we stood, we were booted from the Olympic Village by the US Olympic Committee. Avery Brundage gave the USOC an ultimatum: kick out Carlos and Smith or the whole team can just take a plane back home. I wasn't even staying at Olympic Village, but Brundage's orders were clearly about more than our Mexico City living quarters. We were to be out of Mexico altogether.

That wasn't the end of the humiliations they attempted to visit upon us at these Olympic Games. Avery Brundage had an ace up his sleeve in the person of a young boxer with all the potential in the world: Big George Foreman. Foreman won the Olympic heavyweight gold medal and then famously bowed, waving that small American flag to all four corners of the ring. This was held up by the media as a brilliant patriotic response to our "black-fisted thuggery." George has said that we had nothing to do with what he did, and maybe in George's mind that's the truth. I don't live there myself. But what is true is how it was interpreted by the world. What is also true is the actual story behind what George did.

The head trainer for the 1968 US Olympic boxing team was a man by the name of Pappy Gault. Pappy Gault was someone I considered a pretty good friend of mine. Pappy approached me after our medal stand protest and said, "John, that was a powerful statement you guys made out there. I can't tell you whether I agree or whether I disagree with it. But what I can tell you is that you're going to have to feed your family and I have a plan to help you do that. You come to the fight tomorrow night with Tommie and with your wives and we'll make sure that on the biggest possible stage, it's seen that you have your support." It sounded good at the time, but then we were kicked out of the Olympic Village and everything was so chaotic, we weren't able to attend. In retrospect it's good we didn't.

I'm not sure whether Pappy knew whether we were actually there or not. I can only assume he knew we'd been hustled out of the country. But his plan was to have us right there in the audience when Big George took out that little flag, and did his four-corner bow. If Pappy's plan had come to fruition, this would have, he probably thought, raised George to practically being Captain America and we would have been further embarrassed in the worst possible way. It would have been almost like a pro-wrestling drama with Tommie and me wearing the black hats.

Even though Tommie and I weren't in attendance, we didn't need to be for Pappy to get his message out there. George was the person who loved his country and loved the Olympics: the "good" black athlete. The crazy thing about this entire media drama is that George and I were very good friends leading up to the games, during the games, and even to this very day, we are very cool with each other. George had issues with a lot of the track athletes because we were all college people and he came from Texas poverty. But we always vibed very smoothly. He has said since that he didn't have that flag and bow because of us at all. He has said that he didn't even know why he had it in his hand. He was just euphoric to have won the gold. But Pappy put the flag in his hand and pushed him out there. If you look at George's face, he doesn't look like a happy man. His face is expressionless, and he has the flag hanging low at first, but then people start going crazy. Then, he starts waving it, and then they really go ballistic. George is a great showman and he showed it all off. George told me years later, "John, I want to thank you," because he's got all this money now, and he was really launched at those games for corporate America as the anti-Smith/Carlos. I said to him, "George, I'm happy for you, man." And it's the truth. I'm happy for him as a man, a brother, and a teammate for all of his good fortune, but goodness gracious, did we pay a price.

The Olympic Village is the community for every athlete competing. It's where you hang out. It's where you see your friends. It's where I was no longer welcome when Avery Brundage loudly and publicly announced that he would be kicking us out. This didn't surprise me at all. They felt like we were rotten apples and we could poison the entire barrel. Then as we were leaving Olympic Village, there was a beehive of media in my face, along with sentries of reporters all armed with video cameras. I'd never seen anything like it. At the time, my wife Kim was trying to get into the Olympic Village to meet up with me, and one of these reporters recognized her as my wife. A hundred reporters ran up to her, and suddenly she was in the middle of something neither of us were prepared for. Kim was a small woman and they were blocking her, jostling her, pulling on her coat, yelling things at her, and she was in a world of fear. I didn't see it happening and Vincent Matthews ran to find me and said, "John, your wife's out there. The reporters have her." My temper was already on a hair trigger. I went outside and waded into the middle of this mess of bodies, tossing people aside until I found my wife. As I pulled her away and walked to the safety of a nearby building with security, I turned around and said to them, "Listen, I'm pretty pissed off with some of you white folks out there now. The next one that takes a camera and microphone and sticks it up in my face, I'm going to knock you down and jump on you like you stole something." Then the media took that and said, "He's going to beat the white world up. He said he wants to 'hit a white person right about now.'" That made the news around the world and all of a sudden, I was this fire-breathing dragon that needed to be slain. People saw the moment when I was angry, but not what they were doing to my wife. There was no context, just the sound bite of me saying something regrettable and giving reality to what they already thought I was. They just ran with that. But they were so physical and so nasty, I would challenge anyone to not do the same. Whenever I hear about some celebrity grabbing the camera of a paparazzi and smashing it to the ground, a small part of me smiles.

At the time I didn't think it would be that big of a deal, but I didn't understand the way one quote could be played and replayed until it created a person I didn't recognize as myself, yet everyone assumed it was who I truly was. At the time, I loved all kinds of white folks. But it was a moment in which I felt like a grizzly bear protecting the momma bear. What they did was no different than poking a bear with a stick, shoving my wife, and then when I went to get her, as they must have known I would, I gave them their quote.

I grabbed Kim's hand and stomped out of the village to make our way to Mel Zahn's villa so we could take a breath and plan our next move, but then we saw something far more upsetting than even the media scrum: Mel's wife had packed our bags and left them outside their house. We were officially unwanted everywhere. We picked up our bags and made our way toward the airport. It was time to go home, but we still needed something—anything—to hold on to because after we did what we did, even home was no kind of shelter from the storm.

Six

■　■　■　■

The Unraveling

The Carlos and Smith families were the evil dragons, cast out of Olympic Village, humiliated by the press, and mischaracterized as wild-eyed revolutionists by the opinion makers But wrapped in this slander was a fiction that's been allowed to stand for decades: the idea that Brundage and the IOC "stripped" us of our medals. It just didn't happen. Brundage certainly put that idea out there. They leaked and publicized the idea with the subtlety of a Sherman tank. To this day, people ask me if I ever got my medal back, as if someone had taken it away from me. Hell no. I made it very clear to the IOC that they didn't give me this medal, I earned it. They could try to come to Harlem or the Bronx to take it back, but I didn't recommend it.

In my mind, they set a standard for Tommie and me to meet so we could earn these medals, and we met every standard. Forget politics. I qualified to make that team. I made the journey to Mexico City. I made it through my rounds. I made it to the finals, and I earned my medal. So when they came back to me after the fact with the arrogant assumption that they were going to take the medals, as some sort of punitive measure, I made clear as day to them that it wouldn't happen. I have the right to give this medal to my kids. I find it unbelievable that people still approach me every day and ask how it felt to be stripped of our medals. I find it unbelievable that for the last forty-three years, they have let this lie linger. It's obvious why: they do it to intimidate other young individuals from ever "pulling a Smith/Carlos."

We were facing a world of hurt back home. The *Los Angeles Times* said we had engaged in a "Nazi-like Salute." *Time* referenced our "ugly" gesture on its front cover. The worst was Brent Musburger. He called us "black-skinned storm troopers." As a reward for doing that, the powers that be rocketed him up the ladder to serious fame.

But there were bright spots even in those difficult times. In the media, one exception was Shirley Povich of the *Washington Post*. Povich was a man who had a strong moral voice. He wrote, "If it is unpatriotic in the view of most observers, the courage and dignity of their revolt gesture was inescapable. The mild revolutionists are rare." That meant more than he ever possibly could have known. There were other moments springing from the athletes that gave us a sign that it wouldn't all be in vain. Of course, the best moment, as I mentioned earlier, was when we heard that Wyomia Tyus, speaking for the women sprinters, dedicated their gold medals to us. That was an education right there. Honestly, it was uplifting and downright humbling that they had the courage to give their support. It was uplifting because everyone else had run away from us. It was humbling because they were very much shut out of the process of building the OPHR. I had felt over the last year that we should have been doing much more to involve women in the OPHR but it was like a restricted men's only club and it was established as such before they brought me on board. It made no sense to me. We said we were fighting for all African peoples, but we made no effort to bring our sisters into the fold. The women were shut out. One runner, "Racey" Lacey O'Neal said years later, "They were talking boycott. We were wondering, where was our girl-cott?" The absence of these strong women made us weaker. So when Wyomia and her team came out and made that statement and dedicated those medals to us, we were just humbled and tickled pink at the same time. Years later, Wyomia took OPHR to the woodshed, saying, "It appalled me that the men simply took us for granted. They assumed we had no minds of our own and that we'd do whatever we were told." She was right to do it.

The other moment that gave us a lift in those dark times was the statement from the Harvard crew team. People have asked me often if their support shocked us. But Harvard, believe it or not, was a radical place in those days. At the time, no one was surprised that an elite Ivy League school would have rowers down for the cause. That was just part of what it meant to live in 1968. The crew team wasn't made up of right-wing or conservative individuals. They were free-spirited. They were more like the hippies with no desire and no care for careers as professional athletes. They said that they weren't concerned about reprisal for their political beliefs or their spiritual beliefs so they were just like us. They felt like, whatever the consequences, we needed to come together to do the job. They had been with us all along, giving us their thumbs-up and full support. That support lasted through the years. Before I left for Australia to be a pallbearer at Peter Norman's funeral, one of those old rowers, in an act of true generosity, gave me his OPHR badge so I could place it on Peter Norman's coffin.

But all that took place after we were kicked out of Olympic Village and we were back in the States. Going home had its own set of concerns:

concerns about violence against our persons and concerns about having some kind of network of support. At the time, Kim and I were living in California because I was trying to get with the San Jose State track program. This wasn't Harlem of course, and that put another layer of worry on whether we would be shunned. But our neighbors on Reed Street hung a sign outside our house that read, "Welcome Home John Carlos, Our Hero." That felt really good. It said that no matter how angry the United States was as a whole, the people who knew us knew that our hearts were in it for the greater good. But once you got even five minutes from our neighborhood, you realized that our home block would be the profound exception. The atmosphere was just thick with resentment, anger, and an unhinged fury.

We should have known it would be bad. In Olympic Village, before we left, we noticed that all the international magazines and newspapers from throughout the world had been removed. It was without question because the IOC didn't want the athletes to see what was being said about what we did. They didn't want us to know that the United States and global opinion were on two opposite sides of the table. The world was giving us all due credit for our courage; there was compassion, understanding, and some kind of intellectual engagement as to why two young individuals might put themselves on the line in such a public way. The US press, of course, did not reflect any of this.

Public opinion, when we made it home, was dramatically against us. The editorial boards of the major papers spoke in unison that we were an embarrassment. We were un-American. We disgraced the country my father was shot at fighting for. But no major media gave us the opportunity to speak our minds and articulate why it was exactly that we did what we did. Everything was framed by what they wanted people to think about us. It was about as objective and unbiased as a press release from the Pentagon. It wasn't just our voices that you never heard. You also didn't get an inkling of the support we had throughout the grass roots in America that said that they understood. When I say grass roots, to be perfectly clear, that means black, white, and brown folks who politically were down with what we were trying to express. Someone having black skin in no way meant they appreciated what we had done. I had certain people tell me that we had set black folks back a hundred years. In other words, John Carlos and Tommie Smith raising their fists rivaled the defeat of Reconstruction in the South and the birth of Jim Crow. It boggles the mind.

As for Kim and me, we just tried to shut all those things out of our minds. We tried to just focus on the greatest asset that we had: each other. I knew that Muhammad Ali's wife, Khalilah, was his pillar of strength when he had his title stripped and was banned from the sport. I leaned on Kim, and maybe I leaned too much. But she was very encouraging of me to get out of the house and not to willingly accept the isolation the powers that be were trying to impose on me.

Tommie and I made every effort to try and speak in front of positive audiences. We wanted to wrap ourselves in support. We went around to as many historically black colleges as possible. We did meetings sponsored by fraternities and sororities. If someone was willing to listen to us with an open mind and a degree of respect, we would go there. The problem was that these places, particularly the historically black colleges, didn't have any money for us other than the fact that once we got there, they would pass the hat around and see what they could collect. It was bare-bones, do-it-yourself speaking. But when we would do an event and even if I had only coins jingling in my pocket, I was honored to have the platform, to take a deep breath, and to express why we did what we did. The fact that they passed the hat also meant a great deal, because, for Tommie and me, money was very scarce. We came back, and we couldn't buy butter to put on our bread, let alone any bread. There was a serious downside, I learned quickly, from speaking at these sororities, however. The FBI started to do something very destructive. We would speak at these sororities, and these young ladies would pose for pictures with us after we'd do our speeches. Then somehow they would send these pictures to my wife with notes that these women who I had never seen before or since were my mistresses. It got to my wife to the point where she was so paranoid, every time I went out the door, it was like I was after some woman. This started the very unraveling of my family.

■　　■　　■　　■

We needed bigger speaking gigs to support our loved ones. But they weren't there. We were the disgrace of America at that particular time, so major institutions didn't want to touch us. Also, the fact that we were athletes had many schools looking at us like we were low, as if we didn't have the capacity to express ourselves. We had to make do with some scant speaking stops and little more than that.

Kim up until this point had been handling the pressure like a champ, but it was during this time, after our medal stand demonstration, when a tremendous amount of pressure came on Kim and started to break her down. I'm sure this strained Tommie's relationship with his first wife as well. For a time, anywhere they went, they were accosted by the press. Back then, these jackals were entirely men, and they had a noted and cruel tendency to try and manhandle women subjects. The reporters would make Kim and Tommie's wife stop and talk to them regardless of whether they wanted to speak with them or not. Kim had done nothing in her life to prepare herself for that kind of treatment. I saw her beginning to unravel before my eyes, and it hurt because I knew I brought this madness into my home.

We now had the madness and little else. I was just a man who had to figure out what to do to fend for his family. The track was the only place where I felt a sense of peace. I can understand why Barry Bonds or Kobe Bryant did some of their best playing with controversy swirling around their heads. Your field of play becomes your refuge where the world makes a degree of sense. That was certainly the truth for me. In the midst of all this chaos and controversy, I had my best year as a runner. I was now at long last officially a part of San Jose State University, "Speed City." It was during that 1969 season when I made my case for the Track and Field Hall of Fame. I tied a world record in the 100-yard dash, running that in 9.1, although there are still people who were there that day with their own timers who swear I ran it in 8.8!

I also won the Amateur Athletic 220-yard contest. But the crowning achievement was leading Speed City—with its remarkable tradition and history of Olympians—to its first NCAA championship. I grabbed the gold, breaking the tape in the 100, the 220, and as a member of the 4x110-yard relay. The cheers and honors were like a tonic. But there wasn't a solitary cent in those days to be earned in track and field so after that season, I walked away from that life forever. I had no choice but to make that decision. My family had trouble scraping together its next meal and that had to be my first responsibility. In 1970, Kim and I welcomed our beautiful boy Malik into the world. Malik was a treasure, but very literally, he was also another mouth to feed. It was time to see dollars come in, to try to move on and keep the past from touching our lives so materially. I had gotten word in 1970 that Tommie's mother had died of a heart attack.

After 1968, she had people sending threatening letters and even dead animals to her house. I knew I had to build up the armor around my own family, especially with caring for Malik being such a high priority. But already the armor had been pierced, no question about it. Kim and I weren't communicating much. She looked shell-shocked much of the time, not believing that our lives had taken this turn.

But when I look back, the number one reason there wasn't a whole lot of communication was that there wasn't time for communication. Anyone who has ever been in a position to have to hustle money to pay the rent or run a gauntlet of challenges just to get some groceries in the house knows what I'm talking about. Both Tommie and I were angry that there were people out there on the radical chic gravy train who were benefiting off our moment with everything from books to posters, but doing nothing to throw even some modest means of support in our direction. There were numerous well-known public figures who had resources, and who supported us in the press, but not in our bellies. I must say that there was one exception to this and that was George Foreman. With no fanfare—and honestly, he probably didn't want any fanfare—George reached out with some dollars at a financial low point for the Carlos family. But other than Big George, it just didn't happen.

By 1969 and into 1970, my life was beg, beg, borrow, and steal. If I had $100, I would leave my family and hightail it to Vegas and hit the crap tables to see if I could score us up some money. I just felt like the hustle was the only way to solve the most immediate problems: food and shelter. The hustle is what I did when I wasn't working. Whatever jobs I had to take, I wasn't too proud or too ashamed to do it. I had a job as a security guard at a nightclub, wearing this brownstone ranger uniform. Many people used to come in the club and say, "Hey! Aren't you John Carlos?" They were shocked that I would be doing work like that. But I did what I had to do. I put out the word that I would take whatever job was necessary to make sure that my family was able to eat. The low point came when I had to chop up our own furniture for our fireplace. That was low. That hurt. I clearly needed a new plan.

In 1970, I tried the NFL. That was another hustle. In track and field at that time, it was all amateur and there was no way to actually make a living so you definitely had a very low ceiling on your career. I felt like I was suffocating because I was so close to the ceiling. There was nowhere else to go. The NFL in those days seemed like a good place to land. The 1970s NFL was nothing like it is today. Not the wages, the size, the players, or the playbooks were anything like they are now. But I knew I could sign with a team and make $25,000 and maybe get some of these dogs off our trail. The slight problem with my plan was that I had zero experience with football. My hands were boxer's hands, like Roberto Duran. But Roberto Duran was called "the hands of stone," remember, and nobody wants a wide receiver with hands of stone. But still, despite the 1968 controversy and despite my lack of experience, there was interest. Why? First of all, I could run 100 yards in nine seconds flat and that's something few others could do. But the real reason is that the NFL has always been league of copycats, and everyone wanted their version of "Bullet" Bob Hayes, the all-pro and future hall of famer with the Cowboys who starred on the 1964 Olympic track team.

I signed a contract with the Philadelphia Eagles because they had a player named Irv Cross who was down with the Black Economic Unions started by Jim Brown, and I knew there would be a core of political support on the team. But political support is one thing. My bigger problem was that I just didn't know the game, and the NFL is hardly the place to learn. It's like going to MIT to learn basic arithmetic. Not smart.

But I signed that contract, which meant I'd lost my track eligibility, and I had to make the best out of the situation. I had to leave my family, go to training camp, and concentrate on sending Kim a check every other week. Training camp was hilarious in retrospect, because not all the NFL guys were that aware of the outside world. They tried to treat me like just another anonymous rookie. They wanted me to jump on the table, dance, sing fight songs, and I felt like saying, "Umm . . . did you cats see the Olympics? The whole black fist thing? Anyone?" I didn't want special treatment, unless not being humiliated or not being treated like a child qualifies as special. I'd been through too damn much to sing for anybody. But once they got to see who I was as a person, then all that began to dissipate and we became a team.

People started to look out for me, which was much needed and appreciated. I remember going into the locker room before my first scrimmage and I was trying to put on my thigh pads and was doing it all wrong. I was just trying to strap them on using instincts and common sense, but I had no clue what I was doing. A couple of the other receivers laughed and said, "Come here, Carlos. Come here. Man, you can't put them pads in there like that. They'll squeeze together the first time you're hit, and you'll cut your balls off." At that moment, I was profoundly grateful for my teammates. Those receivers were part of a crew on the team who looked out for me because of what I had done in 1968 and because of what they knew I had been through.

This crew included some white and Samoan players, but it was mostly my black teammates. Take Jim Throu for one. Jim Throu was a defensive back with the Eagles who came up to me early on and said he'd have my back because he respected and admired me for having the courage to stand up for what I believed in. He said that the vice of racism and sports—hero on the field, nobody off the field—had been the dynamic for some time.

We had a couple of white players who came up to me and said, "Hey, man, you ain't the bad guy that they're trying to make you out to be." So, I started off thinking I would have to be very guarded, but those kinds of things relaxed me and made me feel good about being with them.

I wish this part of my story had a happier ending. I lasted in the NFL for roughly a year and a half. This was just long enough to shred my leg up and give me the limp I carry with me to this day. I didn't play long enough to apply for any kind of benefits so the therapy and upkeep for this broken wheel is on me.

I can still see the moment vividly, like it happened yesterday. Irv Cross and I were running some curl patterns. At that time the stadium surfaces were changing from grass to Astroturf and Philly was no exception.

Prior to taking the field, we did our drills on grass so if I ran a pattern, every time I planted my foot, it would slide on the grass. But practicing on turf was an entirely different animal that I wasn't prepared to tame. Irv threw a curl pattern to me, throwing it a little to the left. I stretched to catch it, and my foot didn't slide on that Astroturf, it locked. Just as I caught the ball, I heard a sound call up to me from my knee, and it said in a voice as clear as Dinah Washington's, "pop-pop." Just like that. After hearing that "pop-pop," I ran several more patterns, perhaps three or four more drills. Then I said, "Irv, my leg doesn't feel right." He said what everyone said back at that time. "Well, go on home and ice it." It didn't swell up and there was no intense pain at the time. It just had a little puff to it. The next day, it was just immobile. I could barely pull myself out of bed, and everyone told me I needed to get it checked out more thoroughly. It was time to see the team doctor.

In the team medical facility, I was with a player named Lane Howell who had been under the knife so many times, his legs had more cracks and creases than a broken windshield. The doctor looked over at Lane and said, "Hey, look at this." Then the doc grabbed my leg and started popping it in quick succession in and out of the socket. I didn't know what was going on but an old hand like Lane knew the score. He and Doc sadly smiled at each other and Lane said, "Johnny, I recommend that you get ready for some serious surgery. Your ligaments are cut. Get ready to go under the knife." I looked at him and said, "What are you talking about, man? These are the fastest legs in the world." He said, "Well, they might not be when you come back."

I had no choice but to have the surgery, and I still believe that the doctor who performed that surgery was an old school butcher, with no handle of the new technology that was emerging at the time. Instead of figuring out how to bond those ligaments together so they would heal, he just clipped them out. Now for the last forty years, my bone has just rested on the cartilage. Every time I move, I feel them grind against each other.

By the time I was upright and able to move, I'd lost my speed. I'd lost my wheels. I'd lost my bearings. It also didn't help that Philly brought in a receiver to compete with me named Harold Carmichael who at 6 feet 6 inches ended up changing the position and being the best receiver in Eagles history. No competition at all. I even said that to the coach. I said, "This is no competition. Carmichael is something special." He shot me a look that said, "No kidding, buddy."

Montreal

I was being released by the Eagles, packing my bags and trying to map out my next move, when I received a call from a guy by the name of J. I. Albrecht, general manager for the Montreal Alouettes of the Canadian Football League. He called me and said that the team would like to have me come up to Montreal, come to camp, and have a guaranteed contract. This was a gift.

I had made probably $35,000 in a year and a half with the Eagles, but I had no prospects to make any more, and that money would have been gone very quickly. Montreal was less money, but it was guaranteed. Also, it was Montreal. This is the most slept-on, beautiful city on earth, in my humble opinion. I've always said that if anybody ever wanted to go to Europe, and couldn't afford it, all they'd have to do is go across the Canadian border to Montreal. Everybody speaks French, a lot of folks speaking it as a first language, and there were rows of clubs that were as cool as can be with people dressed to match. Then I got a chance to actually meet and talk to some of the local people, and they were also very impressive as a group because they treated me like a human being, not a villain. They knew what I did and showed me love. It was like I could breathe again. I went to Mr. Albrecht and said to him that if I made the team, I'd like to be able to have dual citizenship. Albrecht resisted because of the political implication that the team was aiding a rejection of America. But I told him that if he couldn't do that, then I couldn't play there.

He saw I was serious about what I said. So he used his many connections to push through my paperwork. The man was connected. After a couple of phone calls he said to me, "John, I want you to go down to this office and take your wife and your kids." Then, lo and behold, before long I was a Canadian citizen.

This meant I was able to have decent health care for my family, get us checked out and get preventative care. I needed that health care because I loved this Montreal dish called *poutine*—French fries, gravy, cheese and, if you needed your protein, sausage. This was a Montreal specialty and I would eat it up. It was comfort food. But everything was comfort up there. I remember one time I had a plan to travel to Toronto for a track meet. At the time, we had a two-story condo with a patio that you could stand outside on and look out. I remember one winter morning all I could see was white. The snow created a cocoon around our house. Not even the snowplows could get on the streets that day.

We had such a wonderful time up there in Montreal, so at times I didn't give a second thought to San Jose. I never even thought about the warm weather or any of the California flavor. I'm an East Coast guy, by heart, by nature, by blood, by spirit, so for me to be back on the East Coast and see the snow, the cold, and just the different attitude was a blessing for me. It helped me become stronger, to endure a lot of the things I had to endure. That breather in Montreal steeled and reinforced me for the trials still to come. Eventually we had to leave Montreal and go back to the States because my one-legged, hands-of-stone football career was done and I needed to work. I love Canada, but I just couldn't find a means of employment up there that would be suitable for me to support my family. I would always miss my poutine and free health care and my family would always miss the sense of peace we had. But without work, I had no choice but to look beyond the borders.

At first, I tried to hook up with the United States Olympic Committee to become a trainer for the sprinters. Suffice it to say, my application was not well received. I tried and tried and tried and tried, but it just never happened. Then Puma athletics approached me about representing them at the 1972 Olympics in Munich. As a condition, and on Kim's insistence, I asked if they would move my family to Southern California. Montreal was good for our family, but our relationship was seriously hurting. It was a good time for a separation. Kim would go to Southern California, and I would go to the Olympics. I thought this would be good for my head. Besides, after Mexico City, how crazy could Munich be? Lord have mercy, was I about to find out.

The 1972 Olympics

My track career was over. My football career was over. My marriage was careening out of control. But I was able to make a connection with Puma athletic gear and represent them at the 1972 Munich Olympics. Today those Olympics are forever scarred by the hostage crisis involving Palestinian militants and the Israeli wrestling squad. After the smoke cleared, the entire team was dead. But we of course had no wind that such an earthshaking tragedy was going to transpire. I was just there to hand out Puma gear to the athletes and talk up the product. For me it was just a job. But for Avery Brundage and the IOC, it felt like a direct threat, like Puma was just a cover for my nefarious plans to "ruin another Olympics." To make matters worse, a widely read German newspaper asked if they could do a human interest story about the fact that I was over there. I agreed and they dressed me up in a dark cape like I was Black Superman. I thought it was going to be a lighthearted profile. Instead the headline in big letters was, "This Is the Man Who Can Wreck the Olympic Games."

My heart almost fell through my feet when that newspaper hit the streets of Munich. I couldn't care less what Avery Brundage thought, but the head coach of the track team was a man from the University of Oregon, Mr. Bowerman. This was a very good man and I had nothing but respect for him. I hated the thought that he would see that and think I was trying to create any kind of dissension on his team. There were several folks on his squad who were on or around the 1968 team, and I didn't want to be seen as leveraging my connections to cause trouble.

I decided to go directly to Mr. Bowerman and tell him that I wanted no trouble. He was cordial and said to me, "John, my friend. They'll tell the story they want to tell. Better you just stay away from their clutches."

I felt very happy with his response and thought that this would be the biggest drama I'd see over there. I couldn't have been more wrong.

During the Olympic Games back then, there was a tradition of a one-day break during the competition. In 1972, all the countries in the "third world" decided to wear their country's colors and cook a dish that represented their local cuisine. It was the finest feast you ever saw in your life. After a whole lot of talking and eating and feeling good, we looked outside of the village and saw what looked like ten thousand soldiers and tanks with radar equipment on top, and all kinds of heavy artillery. I remember saying to somebody, "Damn, they brought all this shit in because all the black and brown folk decided to have a picnic? Isn't this kind of an overreaction?"

Then word reached us that terrorists had taken the Israeli wrestling team hostage. No one thought this would end well. I had one very dear friend on one of the Bahamian teams who was just shaking. I asked him what was wrong and he said to me, "Johnny . . . one of the Jewish fellas came banging on my door screaming to get in, and I opened the door and pulled the guy in. Then these guys with masks and guns came and said, 'Open the door or we're going to kick this door in and we're going to kill everybody.' And we opened the door and they took him. I'll be seeing his face until the day I die."

My bizarre connection to all this was seeing the news footage and noticing that all the terrorists were wearing Puma gear. They had blended in at Olympic Village by dressing like athletes, and they had gotten the gear from my stand. I remember them walking up to get the free gear and being skeptical because I'd never seen these guys before. I asked them, "What do you do? What sport are you in?" But the Puma people were so geeked about just having people wearing their product around the village that they told me to just give it to them. It's just a bizarre footnote to an awful tragedy that they were carrying out this brazen attack in Puma tracksuits. It was the dark side of globalization in the flesh: anger, horror, violence, dispossession, rage, all clothed in Puma gear.

At this point, everyone in the village was in a state of pure terror. No one knew how many people had infiltrated the quarters, and no one knew if there would be more attacks to come. The director (called "the mayor") of Olympic Village was a friend and he approached me for some emergency assistance. "John, I need you to do me a favor," he said. "There is a disco in Olympic Village. I need you to get everyone here into that disco, and please keep them in there because they got snipers out there." As he was saying this to me, you could even hear those German snipers popping caps, the German secret police coming in, and the helicopters with those big blades, right outside. "You know, regardless of what people might say, man, none of these guys are gonna leave alive," the mayor told me.

With a lot of help, we herded everyone into the disco. I jumped on the microphone and said, "Listen, the wars going on all across this earth have come to Olympic Village. There is no safe place. But the love and the peace that we have right here and right now are going to triumph. Our love is greater than all the ills on earth so all we can do is turn up the volume, party in here, keep the energy going."

We partied like hell in there. The disco had all of these mammoth decorative pillows hanging from the walls. They must have been 15 or 20 feet long. After a long while, they were laid on the ground and things started getting cozy. I know a lot of babies were made that evening. It was a room full of people making babies, while trying to ignore the sniper fire outside.

As for me, all I was doing was trying to make sure people stayed in the discotheque. By the next day, we received word that it was over, and the mayor was right: no one left alive. On television they were saying at first that they had gotten the hostages out, and everyone was safe. But I don't think it was even two hours before they came back and said that everybody on the wrestling team was killed. Everybody. It was so awful. I was weeping. It was so much. It was too much. None of us could understand how anything as small-time as the Olympic Games could continue in the face of such horror.

Then Avery Brundage got himself in front of the cameras and gave his infamous speech. He said the games must go on. He didn't say a single solitary word about the people who had died. Instead he said that the games had been victimized by "two savage crimes," referencing the effort to ban Rhodesia from participation in the games in addition to the hostage tragedy. I wish I was joking. This guy was without shame and maybe he was losing it.

When Brundage called for the Olympics to continue, I didn't like it. And make no mistake, I was not alone. I think that a lot of people were disenchanted and disheartened. Brundage talked a great game about how much he loved that Olympic spirit, but he was also about that Olympic dollar, so he wanted to keep the show rolling.

He also, publicly and privately, equated what Tommie and I did with the deaths in 1972. It upsets me more now than it did then. Then it just felt like it was in line with the kinds of things that these individuals were always saying. They looked for scapegoats to cover their tracks. This was just another shameless excuse to attack us for what we did in 1968.

I wanted to get with Tommie and say something about this, to give some kind of political response. Think about it: you had Avery Brundage putting a mass murder of athletes, a slaughter, on our heads. But it was very difficult in those days to stay in contact with Tommie. Tommie had always been an introvert, and I would say that he's probably more outgoing now than he's ever been. But at the time, he had crawled inside himself and didn't want to do any kind of tandem action with me. As for Harry Edwards, he was a big name now on the speaking circuit, but completely out of the loop of what was happening in Munich. I was on my own.

The other incident that happened at the 1972 games that we were also blamed for was the behavior of Wayne Collette and Vincent Matthews. These were two fine African American track athletes and two fine gentlemen as well. They both made it to the medal stand, with Vinny winning the gold and Wayne taking the silver. But they brought all kinds of hell on their heads for looking angry and nonchalant while the anthem was playing. By 1972, no one wanted to hear that Vinny had to climb over the fence surrounding the track during off hours just to train when he was coming up. He felt, with a lot of justification, that he didn't owe anybody anything, so he stood there and twirled his medal. Wayne Collette, who passed away in 2010, also felt like he didn't owe the IOC anything. They were saying to hell with the nationalism involved in these games, and sometimes I think the world would be a much better place if more people did exactly the same.

Let me also give you a contrast. They ridiculed and punished Vinny and Wayne, but then they made excuses for another Olympian. Dave Wottle won the gold in the 800 meters, but when Dave was standing there wearing his hat backwards during the national anthem, everyone said, "Oh, he forgot to take his hat off." They called him "the hat-wearing hero." They made all sorts of excuses for him. And I'm not saying anything bad about Dave because he was a nice individual as well, but I'm just talking about how they put the two together. There was this paranoia or fear of the "angry black athlete." This is what they wanted to portray, and if there is one lesson I've learned through the decades, it's that the media in this country is like the ring in the bull's nose: all you have to do is grab the ring and pull it whichever way you want to pull it, and the general population (if there aren't big struggles going on to inspire us and get us out of our seats), will follow. So, if they write "John Carlos walked on water" in the *New York Times*, you can go to the *Los Angeles Times*, and they'll write, "Reports have been confirmed that John Carlos has in fact walked on water." I could be standing right there, arguing that while such words are flattering, this is just not the case, and they'd say, "Well, the *LA Times* and the *New York Times* said it, therefore it must be so." The media had decided that Vinny and Wayne weren't worth a damn and had nothing interesting to say and therefore that became the truth. But if they hadn't done what they did, I don't think you would have seen the African countries come together in 1976, under the leadership of the South African poet and activist Dennis Brutus, and demand that apartheid countries remain exiled from international sport. In other words, people like Vinny and Wayne kept the spark alive and reminded people that all was not well. Remember, you had Avery Brundage saying it was a "crime" that Rhodesia wouldn't be joining the festivities, so it was Dennis Brutus who took it to the next level and got all the African countries to say that apartheid countries would forever be a part of the Olympic past.

1972 was also the year when we looked at one another and said with pride and defiance that we are one as African people, and that there is no track and field without us—from the USA to the motherland. We dominated the sprints from a half mile down. We had fused and become one and insisted that even Avery Brundage listen to our concerns. And it made a difference. There were also many people around Brundage and in the IOC who were glad we did what we did because it raised awareness about the lack of black coaches and Brundage's shameful, prejudicial practices. I found out about these silent supporters at the IOC later that year when

I was at the Pan Am Games and I was walking with the legendary sprinter Wilma Rudolph. Someone tried to mug us, and I put him down on the street. After we cleared it up with the police, some veteran Olympic officials came up to me and thanked me for protecting Wilma. Then they said, "And thank you for standing up in 1968." This was followed by an awkward silence and then they scurried off. Mercy me, I really wish I had that on tape.

1973

Times were tough back home. I still couldn't make a dime. Kim was hating me, hating life, and constantly in a state of anger or depression. Malik and Kimme had to hear in school that their father was some kind of villain because of 1968. It wasn't even that they heard this from classmates. It came right from the mouths of their teachers.

Every time that happened, I felt rage in a way that reached into my heart, grabbed those "best angels of my nature," and knocked them out. I would go down to whatever school they were in and get right in the teacher's face, male or female. It never became physical, but I made it perfectly clear that whatever differences they had with me, that's where it should lie—with me, not with my kids. I had to put more than a few teachers on notice that if it happened again, they would face a world of problems.

I tried to keep my kids sheltered from this dark cloud of money problems, Kim's depression, and my political shadow, and give them as normal a life as I could. There were times when getting toys for Christmas meant going to the mission. There were times when dinner meant oatmeal and cream of wheat. The lack of money translated into an unbearable tension inside our family. What was once a refuge had become a pressure cooker. When something was broken, we couldn't fix it. We were living on one steady income and it was from my wife, Kim, who was working as a secretary. I remained at a point of beg, borrow, or steal. We also couldn't save a penny because everything that came in flowed right back out to pay bills. I started to gamble more to try to parlay the little we had into something more, but as the saying goes, there's a reason those casinos look so nice.

Depression hit me badly during that period. It was like having "the bear" jump on me when running track. The difference was that instead of feeling the physical rigor mortis, it was mental. It reached the point where I was just got tired of trying. I was tired of every day being a fight. Every day was like going into a burning forest with a water gun.

Yes, I reached the point where I didn't want to get out of bed in the morning, but I will swear on a stack of Bibles that even at the lowest of moments I never had any regrets about what we did in 1968—not even when times were the darkest. I suffered because I just felt really bad for my family. It was my choice, not theirs, to do what I did on that medal stand, but they still had to take the weight. That haunted me. There were people in the world of track and field and the USOC who suggested to me that if I apologized or publicly recanted, certain doors might become open for me to coach or find work. But my attitude was that I couldn't say I'm sorry for doing the right thing.

On one particularly low day, I received a telegram absolutely out of the blue from Ted Kennedy. He told me that he knew what it felt like to face dark times, but I had no reason to be ashamed of what I did. He just wanted to say that I should stand tall and be proud.

This really mattered to me. His brother Robert had been killed on my birthday and was part of that 1968 tapestry that made us feel like we had to do what we did. When I received that telegram, I felt like a drowning man with rocks in his pocket, and Ted Kennedy cut me some holes, allowing me to float to the surface. He gave me hope. He gave me the belief that I was right and I should keep fighting for justice and equality. It was a simple act because we had never met, but I just can't tell you how much of a relief it was for me to read it and see who sent it. It also cleared my head to deal with not only what was happening to my family in the outside world, but also the terrible drama unfolding in our home.

My marriage was breaking up in terribly ugly fashion. It was more than the frustration and lack of money that wore on our household. I wasn't faithful and I take responsibility for that and have my regrets. As I mentioned earlier, someone, most likely the FBI, would send pictures to my wife of me with random young women whom I didn't know or had never met, saying that I had been unfaithful with this one or that one. None of what the FBI was saying was true. The state took her fragile mental condition and put her through hell. Please understand that I'm not trying to say that I was an angel, because I wasn't one, but I was far from the devil that they were trying to make me out to be. I thought in 1968 I could take anything they shot at me and shake it off. But when it hit my family so directly, it knocked me out of the box for good. It was 1973 and I was lost. I went up to Canada to try and play football again, but I didn't stay long. One morning, I called to speak to my kids early in the morning and I just knew something was very wrong. I knew it. I flew home and sure enough, Kim had moved out without telling me. There was nothing left in the house but a barstool, a coffeepot, and the lightbulbs. Everything else was gone. This was depression round two. I remember sitting on that barstool, making a cup of coffee, staring out the window, and wondering what in the world I was going to do.

My life was a world of hurt, but I knew I wasn't alone. This was a period in the 1970s when the movement was clearly beginning to decline. Angela

Davis was arrested. Fred Hampton was killed. The Panthers were fracturing. Many of the 1960s fighters were falling prey to drugs or mental illness. This was no accident. It was part of the government taking back what we had won. When the government decided it was going to go after figures who were against the establishment, they went out to get them. They had a machinery. We had no machinery. Everyone had a feeling like, "Maybe I shouldn't go outside today." I felt that too. I felt, as all these folks were getting beat down, that my suffering was a part of that. I realized that it was happening to all of us. But as I said, who do we run to? Where do we get support or shelter? So all you can do is basically cover your own ass as best you can.

That particular moment was the start of the second stage in my life. I remember going into the living room, sitting down near the window, and I saw the FBI agent who followed me around, drinking coffee in the rain. I was so lonely and so lost, I invited him inside to have a hot cup. He said the rules of surveillance dictated that he was not permitted to actually enter my house and have coffee with me. I asked if it was against regulations for me to bring two hot cups out to the car, and he paused and said no. That's how I found myself cutting against my own isolation and loneliness by drinking some java inside the car of a Fed who had been tailing me. I made conversation, but one question he didn't answer was why he was following me in the first place. It baffled me. My gut reaction was, first of all, to protect my family, because they were following me every day, every which way. But the thing that had me torn up inside was: why? What did I do to deserve them following me everywhere? The only conclusion I could draw was that it was to punish me, to beat me down and to drive me to some point of insanity.

That was a low point and it forced me the next day to start taking some steps out of the hole where I lived. I was in the house the next day, with my barstool and coffeepot, listening to jazz on a transistor radio. I was feeling so sorry for myself, I couldn't even look at my reflection in a puddle. Then I caught myself and said, "Man, life ain't over for you."

These were my darkest days: not having access to my babies Kimme and Malik, hearing them say that they wanted to live with me, having people express their concerns about Kim's mental state, trying to make enough money to send her some.

Then in 1977, Kim took her own life. Even though we'd been apart for four years, I've never been the same since. Malik and Kimme were of course changed forever. They were forced to come to grips with thoughts and emotions children should never have to wrestle with. It also put a lot on my head because now it was on me to raise them correctly and to protect them from all that was evil in the world. Today, they ask me why I took such great pains to shield them from a lot of the ugliness on this planet. I say, "Hey, my job was to make sure you were healthy and happy, that you had food in your bellies and that you were going to school to get your education. That was my job—to protect you and watch over you the best that I could. Anything outside of that, you'll learn soon enough."

I didn't want my kids growing up with unfocused anger coursing in their veins about anything. I wanted them to have an even playing field where they didn't have any hostilities in their lives. Today we are all independent and everybody is doing their own thing and I couldn't be prouder.

Seven

■ ■ ■ ■

Efforts at Resurrection

As the 1970s came to a close, the people in and around my life still treated me like I had leprosy. I could see the fear people had for just being associated with me or with my kids. Of course, because of my persona and the way I carried myself, I didn't exactly invite a great deal of company. I'm a happy-go-lucky guy most times, but I've also got something of a rough edge that in those days was standing straight up against my back. By 1980, it was Reagan's America and no one wanted to see a dragon past his day. Reagan wanted to erase the 1960s. I've always thought that my isolation was collateral damage in a much larger process.

I wasn't hating people. I was just bearing down. This was like a football game. Maybe I was down 50 to nothing in the first half. But I said to myself, "Thank God there's a second half. If I kick ass and take names, the second half is mine."

I was alone, but able to rebuild at least the beginnings of a foundation for a life. I entered something called the Seeder Program, which aimed to place low-income, underprivileged individuals like myself in temporary jobs that hopefully would turn into permanent jobs. This might sound humbling, but I've never for a solitary moment been afraid of hard work. I was placed as a caretaker in San Pedro Park, down by the docks of Los Angeles, trimming trees, pulling weeds, and making sure it was up to snuff. I was making sure that everything would be tip-top right in front of General San Pedro's house. It was hard work, no question, but I needed to send money to my kids, keep my head clear, and rebuild. The hard physical work may have kept my mind fresh, but it made my bones ache, especially the knee I left on the artificial turf of Philadelphia.

One day I was down on the ground cutting the grass and pulling the weeds, and I saw at my eye level these baggy, furry, red pants and big shiny black boots. I looked up from the ground, and saw this big belly hanging down over me. The belly was so huge I looked up and I couldn't see the man's face. All I could hear was this voice saying, "What are you doing down there, 'Los?" I sat back on my heels, looked up, and it was my friend, the former football player Rosie Grier.

Rosie was of course dressed up like Santa Claus with this big, fake belly. He was down in San Pedro cheering up the kids at Christmastime, and he had gotten word that I was down there on my knees working on my calluses. I looked up at him and smiled—because it was impossible to be around big Rosie without smiling—and I said, "Rosie, I gotta do what I gotta do, man. I gotta support my family." He said, "Listen, given the price you've paid, we can do better. I'm going to give you a phone number." I took this phone number from Rosie, thinking it would be to get a job as a store manager or something of that nature. But when I looked at the card, I saw that it was the private number of the mayor of Los Angeles, Tom Bradley. Well, all right then. I called the number after work and the next thing I knew, I was sitting down with the mayor. Bradley was very gracious and quite the fan of what went down in 1968. After we spoke, he called a member of the Los Angles City Council named Dave Cunningham. Dave hired me to work for him, to use my mind, to help hear the concerns of the community, and to be a public figure in his area.

I think that was the first time since 1968 that I was able to actually touch ground with my feet. It wasn't just because I was finally getting a steady check. It wasn't just because I could finally put the temp work of the Seeder Program behind me. It was because it allowed me to be a public figure in the community and I found that when I could be open and active among regular people in Los Angeles, I wasn't the fire-breathing outcast. I was somebody people wanted to hear. I felt rebuilt. When I wasn't working for Dave, I had made enough connections to start something called the John Carlos Youth Development League to mentor kids. I applied for grants from the city to help with the work and was told that since I worked for the city, there was a conflict of interest in applying for grants. I had a decision to make and had to decide whether working with kids was far more important than that comfortable steady check.

As I was trying to decide what fork to take in the road, we had a party at Dave Cunningham's office for a coworker who was retiring. I felt compelled and inspired at that moment to stand up and say that after two years, I was "retiring" also—to work for these kids. I had just seen too many programs that had failed young people and I felt like I could do it right. Regardless of what people thought of me, I felt very strongly about kids getting a good foundation, a real education, and having knowledge of themselves, their history, and the opportunities in front of them. It wasn't easy by a long shot to deal with the city bureaucracy or grants; I toughed it out. We survived, reached a lot of kids, and did OK for ourselves even if it was hardly anything that could generate a real income. But it paid very well in too many other ways to count. These young kids didn't care a lick what I'd done in 1968. Few of them had even been born by 1968. They just cared if you were one of those adults who would listen to them, or one of those adults who would make them feel low down and no good. I listened and for them that was enough.

The foundation work was good for me because it kept me grounded and it ensured that my head remained in a good place. It also gave me some stature. By this time, it became clear that there was a serious effort to get the Olympics to Los Angeles in 1984. The Los Angeles Olympic Committee (LAOC) effort was headed by Peter Ueberroth, another alumnus of San Jose State, who today is the head of the USOC. I approached the LAOC because I was concerned that the young people of LA were going to be shut out of the party. So many of the stadium venues were going to be in the 'hood, but meanwhile the opportunities for youth sports were dwindling. This had to be addressed. I wrote a letter to Peter Ueberroth expressing these concerns. He eventually had the LAOC respond to me, and I had to read their letter three times before I was able to decipher that it was a whole bunch of nothing. I grabbed the phone and called Peter's office again and told them, "This is John Carlos. Your committee sent me this letter, and I am terribly unsatisfied. I think you need to call me right away so I can figure out if these Olympics will give anything back to the community." Peter called me back that day and said, "Damn, John, I figured I better call you myself. I heard you sounded like you wanted to kick my ass."

Peter is smooth like that. He had me laughing and then cut right to the chase and asked me what my concerns were. I said, "Look Peter, all I want is to make sure the LAOC is connected to the community and makes sure that the young people of the community are clued in and included in what's going on. You know and I know that bringing the Olympics to Los Angeles will cause a serious disruption in their lives. Let's give something back." Then I offered to have my youth program facilitate this process. He told me, "Well, listen, I'm going to take all this into consideration and I'll get back to you in thirty days or less." Thirty days came and thirty days went. I didn't hear anything.

Then the personnel director of the LAOC invited me to a baseball game. At the game was a director of Olympic planning, a woman by the name of Priscilla Florence. We had a fine old time and she told me, "Listen, now, Mr. Ueberroth asked me to offer you a job, a formal position with the Olympic Committee." I said, "I'm really surprised because I didn't come here looking for a job. I have a job trying to run my youth program." She said, "Well, this is a good opportunity for you and you should consider it. The job won't be around after the Olympics and your youth program isn't going anywhere." It was a tough decision, but what tipped the scales was my family who said, "This might be a way to get back into the sport on your own terms without having to recant or apologize for anything you did. This might be a turnaround for you." I said, "OK, let's give it a shot." So I went back, accepted the job, and went in. People were very nice and cordial and gave me a degree of respect that I had yet to experience from anyone in the Olympic world since 1968.

The entire 1984 Olympics operation was done in state-of-the-art fashion. Avery Brundage, at long, long last, was out of the picture and in Peter Ueberroth we had someone who undeniably was a very intelligent individual, very charismatic and quite the sharp operator. Peter, even more than Avery Brundage, is responsible for the Olympics we have today. Brundage had that cold war, East-versus-West mentality. Peter saw the commercial potential of the games, all the corporate sponsors trying to get a piece of revenue, and brought them in to underwrite and brand the games. Peter did this outside of the IOC. He got international corporations to take over sponsorship of the games and the LA Olympics were the first games in fifty years to actually pull a profit. That was all because of Peter Ueberroth.

I went about trying to facilitate youth programs with the games, and trying to keep as low a profile as possible. I wasn't going to be posing with any black capes this time. Then Peter told me that he wanted me to be one of the people to run with the famed Olympic torch on its journey to the LA Coliseum. It was a terrific honor and of course I said yes. I was so excited that I went out to the club with my buddies the night before. This didn't seem like a big deal. I knew that I'd just be running no more than 100 or 200 yards. And besides, this was a time for celebration, and you had better believe, celebrate we did.

The next day I got the baton just a little bit beyond La Brea and Slauson going north. I was feeling all the adrenaline. Even my knee for a moment didn't seem to hurt. People were cheering and there was a helicopter flying high overhead; I started putting on a show, waving around the torch, enthusiastic, jumping around like a little kid and not a man pushing forty. I reached the corner and looked for someone to pass the baton to. I saw an official and I asked, "Man, where's the person I'm supposed to pass this to?" He said, "Aw, they didn't tell you? You have to go a mile up that hill!" So, I struggled all the way up that doggone hill and finally passed the torch off. By the time I made it up the hill, the torch was damn near down by my ankles and my knee was grinding in a way I knew I'd feel later. When I was done, I leaned against a wall, and slid down like I was about to die, and all my boys came around. I told them, "Come over here and stand around me and don't let people see me like this." I remember going back to Peter saying, "I'm not going to forget the trick you pulled on me!" He laughed, but I wasn't laughing, believe that.

It felt good to give the young people of LA a taste of the Olympics. But there was this concern swirling around my mind—some of the police crackdowns in Los Angeles were starting to make it into the margins of the newspapers. I'd seen what happened in Mexico City. I knew what could be done to make an area Olympic-friendly. Anybody who looks like a threat by definition is a threat. They are going to get weeded out one way or another. This has now become as much a part of the Olympics as the lighting of that torch. In 1996 before the games in Atlanta, I tried to tell a very good friend of mine down in those parts to watch himself, but he paid me no mind. He later found himself incarcerated, his entire life short-circuited.

When the Olympics ended, I was back in the doldrums again. The Olympic job wasn't permanent and my time away from the youth program had put it on death's door. I got back in touch with Peter Ueberroth and I said, "Man, nothing ever happened. I thought it would lead to something, but it didn't." But I had served my purpose and Peter paid me no mind. I had to work at a grocery store, and I worked at the aluminum mills—I was never too proud to work. But life started to get better because I met the woman who would become my current wife, a beautiful woman named Charlene Norwood. She was—and is—so beautiful and together. Charlene had her own cosmetology business, but even more than that, she understood me. She understood that I had my bouts of depression. She understood that sometimes I needed to talk, sometimes I needed silence, and sometimes I just needed to heal. We joined our two families together, mine and Charlene's, and we've made it work.

As with Kim, money was tight; things would break and we wouldn't have the money to fix them—but here's the difference. One day the lawnmower was broken and of course we couldn't get it fixed and the grass was just out of control. It was like a jungle out there. Now I've got some Oscar Madison in me and I could have ignored it. But Charlene likes things just so and having an Oscar Madison lawn was not an option. One day, Charlene came home from work with a something gift-wrapped for me and I just thought it was a sweet surprise. She said, "I've got a present for you." I looked at her, and said, "Oh, yeah?" And she said, "I got one for me too. Go on and open it." I went to pick it up. It was heavy, but I had no idea what it was. And when I tore the paper off, I saw that it was giant hedge clippers. She said, "Listen, I'm going to get on this end of the lawn and I'm going to start cutting. Go over there to the other side and do the same and one day, we're going to meet up in the middle." This wasn't a joke gift from Charlene. She was serious. This was also probably the greatest therapy in the world for me because every time I would cut the hedges, the bushes, and the tall grass, I would feel the sweat, feel the strength, and feel like I was coming back again. Charlene deserves all the credit. She worked diligently. She took my kids in. She loved them like they were her own. And make no mistake; I wasn't the easiest guy to deal with at that time, with all the wounds that scarred me. So, she had to not only deal with all our kids, but she had to deal with me. It was time to really get it together.

Palm Springs

It started with my kids who always said, "Daddy, let's get out of the city and go to Palm Springs. We hear on television that it's pretty." And I would just look at them and say, "Man, ain't nobody in Palm Springs but Bob Hope and Frank Sinatra and they're not going to roll with your Daddy." But they pushed and we went to check it out. The kids walked around and said, "Its beautiful. It's quiet, clean. There's no helicopter chase, no police chase. The schools are beautiful. We love it." I actually thought I saw some potential there. So I told my Charlene, we'll move there, and stay five years in order for our kids to go to a proper school and graduate. That was twenty-five years ago. It was a godsend for me to end up here. As far as the living conditions here in the desert, it's nice, no more and no less. It's not like it's so wonderful for your social life here in the desert. There aren't a lot of things to do. But once you have a house full of kids you have to decide whether it's going to be an adults' house with kids in it or a kids' house with adults in it. We wanted a kids' house.

I have always been a person, thanks to Earl Carlos, who defined myself by my work, and Palm Springs was a place where I could have a job that made me proud. Palm Springs is populated by more than just old retirees. There's another Palm Springs, and I was trying to help that side of the tracks. I became the guidance counselor at Palm Springs High School and have been for many years now. This has allowed me to work with so many kids over the years and try to give them some sort of foundation of self-respect. I always wanted to help them realize that they're a significant part of this society in which we live, and they have a job to do to be successful in their lives, to obtain their education, to go on and build their families and not waste time going to the penitentiary and making the mistakes that so many others have made in the past.

Every time I hear a kid come back and say, *Mr. Carlos, I just want to thank you*, those are like pennies from heaven for me, like God is giving me rewards for my deeds in life. I don't think there's a better job in the world than trying to communicate to young people and help them see things in a new light. I also have always loved it because I know that they can teach me various things as well.

One of the things about the job that gave me peace was that when I originally came here, much of the faculty didn't know who I was. Many of the students didn't know who I was. But at the same time, there were whispers about me like I was a different kind of cat. Then, one day some kids were cutting out of school and I saw them, told them to stop, but they wouldn't listen. I had to run these kids down. My knee may have hurt, but half of a John Carlos is still something compared to kids. I remember I turned the corner, and they were hiding in the bushes and I heard one of them say, "Man, who is that old man? He sure can run!" I said, "Yeah, he ran fast enough to get you, so come on out of there." They looked at me like I was Spiderman, asking, "Who are you?" I told them that if they had gone to school as opposed to going through school, they might have had the opportunity to learn who I am. I said, "Now you go back and research and find out who I am." I heard no more about it until they were in their history class, and they just so happened to open their book and saw the picture of the demonstration on the medal stand.

It shakes me up that the demonstration is always there in the history books and they have a caption underneath, but they never tell the story. The picture itself is such an eye-opening picture, a stunning picture. Regardless of what era you're from, it'll get your attention because it's so affecting. Many of the kids took note of the picture, and they started reading the caption underneath. It mentioned John Carlos. These particular kids that I caught that day, they started coming around, asking me, "Mr. Carlos, we have this history book, and we see this picture with these guys with their fists up, and this guy has your name. You know anything about that?" I said, "Well, maybe you should go research it some more and come back and we can have a discussion about that." From that point it kind of snowballed and all the kids and faculty began to become aware of my history.

Palm Springs was a blessing because I knew I needed to work with kids and forget about being John Carlos, the Olympian, or John Carlos, the pariah, and just try to make a difference. My theory about working with kids is something that I once heard from a Baptist minister in church: he said that he would try to save one soul, knowing that he'd save more than one, but that he'd work that day just to save one. That's the approach I try and take with kids. I don't ever go into it saying, "Oh, I'm going to save all these kids." I'm just looking to get that one. And nine times out of ten, I'm going to do better than that, but the focus is that one kid. Over a period of time you have kids giving their thanks, appreciation, love, and respect. You hear things like, "If it wasn't for you, I'd be dead, in jail, or strung out on drugs, and I'm going to law school now" or "I'm in medical school or a nurse." Those are the tangible things that you take with you when you're trying to get into heaven. I guess those are the things that you point to and say, "Well, Lord, here's my resume."

That's the way I size it up because I'm serious about the work that I do. If I have to deal with a kid's parents, I'm going to deal with that. If I have to deal with the administration, I'm going to deal with that. If I have to deal directly with a kid, I'm going to deal with that. I'm just going to make it possible for every kid I come in contact with to have the opportunities I was trying to provide for my kids: a level playing field where they can take off and try to be in life who God intended them to be.

Eight

■　■　■　■

Save Your Redemption

I was happy being in Palm Springs, being anonymous, caring for Charlene, my family, and the kids at the school. That was enough for me. As I've said, I accepted the fact that people would treat me not like a hero but like a survivor, like I survived cancer. If that was going to be life, then that would be fine. Every once in a while something would happen that made people dig me up and want to talk to me, but mostly, I sent people away. There were documentarians, and people talking movie deals, even people who wanted to give awards, but I wanted nothing to do with it. The only time I felt the old buzz would be when the media would contact me because someone was, in their words, "pulling a Smith/Carlos." In 1996, when NBA guard Mahmoud Abdul Rauf entered a world of pain because he didn't want to stand for the national anthem, they dug me up. When a young lady basketball player, Toni Smith of Manhattanville College, in 2003 decided that she wasn't going to face the flag before games to protest the wars in Iraq and Afghanistan, they found me. I remember seeing reports on her and thinking that there are certain blades of grass that God put on this Earth, and that young lady was a special blade of grass—like Dr. King and Malcolm, like Tommie Smith and Muhammad Ali. This young lady was that type because she had the fiber to stand up against all odds for what she believed to be true. Like anybody who stands in that vein—it takes a number of years to go by before people realize that that young lady was right in what she did.

But I didn't really start to get out of my shell until 2005. That's when I received word that San Jose State was commissioning a statue of Tommie Smith and me for the campus. But what was truly special was not the statue, but how it came about. Tommie and I were hardly the most popular people among board of trustee types, even after all these years. But the students on campus organized a movement that made the statue happen. They were challenged by a professor named Cobie Harris. The students weren't even aware that Tommie Smith and I were alumni of the school until Cobie taught them this piece of San Jose State history. Cobie put it to the students, telling them that if they wanted to see this legacy honored, they would have to do it themselves. Sure enough, the students raised $380,000 to have it built. The faculty and the administration had nothing to do with it. The students felt that this was something they wanted to do. I was elated—to have a statue created and placed at your alma mater is a special honor. But we also got more than statues.

I made a proposal to the people at San Jose State. I asked them to go back and tell the faculty, the student body, or whomever, that I would like to see them bestow honorary doctorate degrees on Tommie and me. There was skepticism from the people I spoke with, but I told them that if the Smothers Brothers, also alumni of San Jose State, could be awarded honorary degrees because they were comedians, Tommy Smith and John Carlos deserved no less. To me, the "Dr." in front of my name was important because I was dyslexic as a young man, and now I spend my days talking to kids about education. I wanted them to know it could be done. Happily, my San Jose people came back and said they could do it.

When I first saw the design of the statue, I had a problem with it because the sculptor left out my brother from another mother, Peter Norman. Remember, Peter was hardly passive in 1968, and he paid a helluva price upon his return. But the sculptor Ricardo Gouveia, who went by the name of Rigo 23, did this so people could climb up on the medal stand with us and do everything from pose for pictures to lead speak-outs. When Peter heard about it, he thought the concept was just fantastic. "I love that idea," said Peter. "Anybody can get up there and stand up for something they believe in. I guess that just about says it all." When he said that, it made him even larger than life—in my mind and in my heart—than ever before.

This Rigo 23 fellow also did an amazing job on the details. Everything from the color and texture of our uniforms, to the expressions on our faces, to our shoeless feet, to the beads, to my open jacket, to the angle of our fists—it just makes me proud because you can learn the history from just looking it over.

"Will Smith and Carlos only be stone-faced amidst a beautiful plaza?" Professor Ethel Pitts-Walker asked the crowd. "For them to become immortalized, the living must take up their activism and continue their work."

2008

As the fortieth anniversary of our time on the medal stand approached, reporters and television shows started to beat down our doors to get comments. The hook was also the Olympics going to China. People always asked, "Do you think any US athletes will 'pull a Smith/Carlos' to protest China?" I said, "Man, we didn't go to Mexico City to protest Mexico! Courage is telling the world you have to get your own house in order. That's responsibility number one." But the crazy thing was that people really wanted to hear what I had to say. I didn't feel like the "cancer survivor" that no one wanted to make eye contact with anymore. People were taking a serious look at the substance of what we were standing for back then, and they gave us love for it. After all, we wanted Muhammad Ali's title restored. We wanted more black coaches. We wanted apartheid South Africa and Rhodesia excluded from the games. We wanted Avery Brundage gone. That was dynamite back in 1968, but it all looks pretty damn good now. It's like that Gandhi quote: "First they ignore you, then they ridicule you, then they fight you, then you win."

It was simply fantastic to finally feel the embrace. But I couldn't help but notice at the same time that the media kept trying to put a divide between what we did then and its application to today. They wanted it to be all about "those tumultuous days way back when." I wanted to say that the Olympic movement still needs work. I wanted to say that the way the poor folks were treated in Atlanta in 1996, the way the people were kicked out of their homes in Beijing, shows that we still have battles to fight. I wanted to say that this was a problem that needs to be addressed. But with only a few exceptions, that's when they turned the cameras off.

The ultimate moment that made my head spin was in 2008 when ESPN, an organization that tends to be very critical of modern athletes who speak out on politics, gave Dr. Smith and me the Arthur Ashe Freedom Award at their awards show, the ESPYs. There were two problems for me in accepting this honor. My first reservation was that Brent Musburger was on ESPN's payroll. I couldn't stand the hypocrisy. They wanted to honor us for our courage and the stand we took, but they felt like it was smart business to handsomely pay a man who called me a "black-skinned storm trooper" just because I felt that it was my right to stand up against the injustices that black people and other minorities faced around the world. I had serious doubts about whether their commitment was genuine or whether we were just going to be figureheads. But my family told me that I needed to go through with it, and that rejecting the award because of Brent Musburger was old stubborn John, not new and improved John.

The other barrier in accepting the award had to do with problems between Tommie and me. At that time Tommie and I were experiencing a great deal of friction. He had written a book saying some uncharitable things about me—and I have a lot of pride. We weren't appearing together at events, and we had stopped speaking. The *New York Times* even wrote about what a tragedy it was that on the fortieth anniversary of a moment that symbolized unity, we were apart. But when ESPN came to us, both Tommie and I realized that the whole anniversary year was bigger than us. We didn't own this moment anymore. It belonged to everyone, and we had an obligation that went along with that.

When we finally came out on stage to receive the award, I think it shocked people to see all the athletes in the audience give us a standing ovation, but I wasn't surprised. All these young football, basketball, and baseball players, who heard about us from their parents, have always showed us respect, admiration, and pride for who we are, what we fought for, and why we did it. They've given us a thumbs-up, and they know we paid a tremendous price. At the same time, as subtle as it may be, they make you aware that what they have today is a result of what we did yesterday. It's always a rewarding feeling. It's not tangible money that I can put in the bank, but to me it's as good or better than money to receive accolades from the younger generation. It lets me know that what I did years ago took root.

ESPN then approached us about doing a special where they would fly us to Mexico City to "the scene of the crime," so to speak. They took us back to the hotel room and we had flashbacks of the media charging in our room. They interviewed us about the details of what we went through. They wanted me to go down to the village and reflect on where my wife was almost trampled by the press, and where she almost slapped a reporter who has leaning on her. They wanted us to walk through the training area and go in the stadium. It was one of the most intense experiences of my life, in some ways more intense than 1968 itself. I said before that that stadium was like a living organism in 1968, and I believe that it is still a living, breathing organism. So many world records were set in that stadium. So much controversy was sparked in that stadium. So much blood was shed right outside its doors. All that was part of the energy held captive by that arena. And after all these years, it still thrummed.

I felt the vibrations and I realized that even as I face my seventieth birthday in the near future, I still feel the old impulses, the old compulsions, to stand up and be heard, no matter the cost, no matter the price. I still have fire inside me that I just don't talk about. I still don't think that I'm where I need to be or should be or could be in my life. I think as well as I've worked with kids, there are things I don't think that I had the opportunity to do in this life. I think God had intentions for me to do more, but yet still I hear the breath of God telling me, "You did more than most people ever thought you would be able to do under the circumstances, so just keep on keepin' on and we'll see what comes." When I hear that voice, I tell God politely that he sounds too much like the devil for my taste. The struggle doesn't end for me. It's like being a war veteran who has come home. You're looking good, you're feeling good, but the minute you sit down and think, you start having flashbacks: flashbacks that napalm your brain. There are just certain things that are not going to go away. But when you hit the streets and try to make the world a little more fair for the next person, the demons are pushed aside. For one night, at least.

Afterword

■   ■   ■   ■

Dave Zirin

John Carlos represents the best in the traditions of sports, politics, and resistance. As the movements of the 1960s faded and the forces of reaction had their day, this tradition was cut off at the knees.

Now it's being reborn, as the movements are reborn as well. As I write this, I'm returning from rallies of up to seventy thousand people in Madison, Wisconsin, against Governor Scott Walker's assault on the rights of public-sector workers. The protests were given a lift by the team that just won the Super Bowl: the Green Bay Packers.

The world is changing.

The Packers are more than just the closest thing the state has to an official religion: they are the only nonprofit, fan-owned team in all of major US professional sports. This is a team with a hundred and twelve thousand owners. When they won the Super Bowl, their coach, Mike McCarthy, said, "We're a community-owned football team, so you can see all the fingerprints on our trophy."

As the protests gained momentum, several players took the Green Bay ethos to heart and immediately backed the workers. Current players Brady Poppinga and Jason Spitz and former Packers Curtis Fuller, Chris Jacke, Charles Jordan, Bob Long, and Steve Okoniewski issued a joint statement that reads:

> We know that it is teamwork on and off the field that makes the Packers and Wisconsin great. As a publicly owned team we wouldn't have been able to win the Super Bowl without the support of our fans. It is the same dedication of our public workers every day that makes Wisconsin run. . . . But now in an unprecedented political attack Governor Walker is trying to take away their right to have a voice and bargain at work. The right to negotiate wages and benefits is a fundamental underpinning of our middle class. When workers join together it serves as a check on corporate power and helps ALL workers by raising community standards.

Rookie tight end Tom Crabtree tweeted, "i fully support wi unions and i think Gov. Walker is out of his damn mind."

None of these players have a particularly high profile. But as the struggle intensified, the team's defensive captain, Charles Woodson, couldn't stay silent. Woodson's words also mattered because he was one of the two reps for the NFL Players Association at a time when the players' union was facing the prospect of an extended lockout. A former Heisman trophy winner at the University of Michigan, NFL defensive player of the year, and perennial pro-bowler, Woodson is also the team's co-captain and union rep. His words landed in sports pages around the country:

> Thousands of dedicated Wisconsin public workers provide vital services for Wisconsin citizens. They are the teachers, nurses and child care workers who take care of us and our families. These hard working people are under an unprecedented attack to take away their basic rights to have a voice and collectively bargain at work.

It is an honor for me to play for the Super Bowl Champion Green Bay Packers and be a part of the Green Bay and Wisconsin communities. I am also honored as a member of the NFL Players Association to stand together with working families of Wisconsin and organized labor in their fight against this attempt to hurt them by targeting unions. I hope those leading the attack will sit down with Wisconsin's public workers and discuss the problems Wisconsin faces, so that together they can truly move Wisconsin forward.

Immediately, across online message boards came the familiar notion that he should just "shut up and play." As one person wrote, "Stay out of it, Charles. Keep your mouth shut and do what you do best—just win." But as Woodson must realize, and as the august message-board commenter clearly does not, this isn't a moment for any pro football player to just know his place and shut his mouth. It's about the solidarity that both sides desperately need. Two very different workforces are both facing battles for their respective futures against bosses that see them as expendable. It's a twenty-first-century fight from the governor's office to the gridiron.

The world is changing.

I spoke with DeMaurice Smith, the head of the NFL Players Association (NLFPA), and he also gave words of solidarity: not just to the workers of Wisconsin but to the workers of Egypt. "You know," he said, "we watched things unfold in a far-off country where a lot of the discussion preceding the protests was purely social media, people connecting. We have an ability to get our 'let us play' ad out. We know that anybody listening can type in 'let us play' and that ad will pop up and, frankly, if networks want to make a decision to boycott us, keep us off, those are the kind of things that get me fired up and let me know that I'm on the right side of right."

The events in Egypt clearly put wind in Smith's sails. And why not? After all, NFL commissioner Roger Goodell seems much less intimidating when compared to former Egyptian president Hosni Mubarak. As Smith said, "There are some socially and politically significant things occurring in the world that don't have anything to do with the final score. So the other day I was with [Baltimore Ravens player] Dominique Foxworth, and he said,

> "I've just been glued to what's been going on in Egypt and the way in which ordinary people are taking a stand against what they feel is oppression." And let's get it clear, those folks are risking everything to take ownership of what their lives are going to look like. This is also Black History month. That's the time to remember and reflect that people across the generations have historically taken stands and been willing to risk everything for causes that they deem are important. The Founding Fathers who signed the Declaration of Independence knew that if they lost, they had signed their own death warrants with their names on that document. Well, that's the spirit of our country and I dig it. And no, I don't want to equate what [the NFLPA] is doing on that scale, but what I've asked our players to do is to recognize their place in history in this fight for a new collective bargaining agreement. . . . You have to realize that there is a solid line between the players of the past and those today who are leaders in this fight.

There is a social movement unionism aspect to how Smith is running this negotiation that stands apart from any sports labor conflict we've seen since the days of Curt Flood, the Major League baseball star who sacrificed his career to win free agency and refused to be, as he put it, "A well-paid slave." The NFLPA had taken part in press conferences with low-wage stadium workers in Detroit who would find themselves locked out if there were no games this fall. I asked Smith if this was aimed at placing pressure on Goodell and the owners by highlighting the predicament of thousands of workers who would be hurt by a lockout. He responded:

I don't know if it places pressure on him or not, whether it places pressure on the owners or not, and frankly, I don't care. This is what we do. The business of football means that there's over 150,000 people who work in [businesses connected to game day during the season]. Whether it is car services, food services, trash removal, the moving of people to and from the game, the money in the bars and the restaurants, the hotels . . . this is the business of our business. So if you draw a circle around football it's a $9 billion entity inside the circle. When you draw the concentric circle outside of football it's got to be in the $20 to $30 billion range. So to say that we can live, work, and operate in a world where we can intellectually or morally divorce ourselves from everything that's going on outside of our circle, you can't, you simply can't.

The world is changing.

Then there are attacks on immigrants, and the athletic response. On Cinco de Mayo in 2010, the NBA's Phoenix Suns went where no American sports team has gone before: they took a political stand. The squad from Phoenix took the court in their playoff game against the San Antonio Spurs, wearing jerseys that read simply Los Suns, coming out as one against Arizona's Senate Bill 1070, aimed at criminalizing anyone suspected of being an undocumented immigrant. This was the first time in US history that an entire team—from owner to general manager and players—had expressed any kind of unified political stance.

As team captain Steve Nash said, "It's racial profiling. Things we don't want to see and don't need to see in 2010." All-Star power forward Amare Stoudamire, who unlike Nash has no political reputation, also chimed in, saying, "It's going to be great to wear 'Los Suns' to let the Latin community know we're behind them 100 percent."

The audacious move by the Suns was simply the most public manifestation of a low-frequency sea change in the world of sports, where more and more athletes are using their hyper-exalted, brought-to-you-by-Nike platform, to say something more than "We just play one game at a time . . . good lord willing."

For most of the last fifteen years, Michael Jordan's famous 1995 statement that "Republicans buy sneakers too" has been the guiding principle of the modern athlete. From Peyton Manning to Derek Jeter, the dominant message has been that it's far more important to be a brand than a man, and a modern jock should never sacrifice commercial concerns for political principle. As former boxing champion George Foreman, the man with the golden grill, once told me, "The political stuff can be for after we retire."

But with SB 1070 signed and sealed by Governor Jan Brewer, the Suns felt like they didn't have the luxury to wait. They were also pushed by numerous Major League Baseball players expressing their anger with Arizona's laws, as well as an emerging movement to move the 2011 Major League All-Star Game from Phoenix in protest. With a large proportion of players and fans from Latin America or of Latin origin, SB 1070 and the politics of division unleashed by it has raised the racialized specter of an All-Star game haunted by four words: "Show me your papers."

Already twenty MLB players have spoken out against the bill. "If they happen to pull someone over who looks like they are of Latin descent," said Rod Barajas, catcher for the Mets, "even if they are a U.S. citizen, that is the first question that is going to be asked. But if a blond-haired, blue-eyed Canadian gets pulled over, do you think they are going to ask for their papers? No." Michael Young of the Texas Rangers added, "You can quote me. It's a ridiculous law. And it's an embarrassment for American citizens."

San Diego Padres All-Star first baseman Adrian Gonzalez and Chicago White Sox manager Ozzie Guillen have said that they intend to boycott the game. Kyle McClellan of the St. Louis Cardinals said, "The All-Star game, it's going to generate a lot of revenue. Look at what it did here for St. Louis. It was a huge promotion for this city and this club and it's one of those things where it's something that would definitely leave a mark on them if we were to pull out of there. It would get a point across."

This was only the latest example of a sports world unable to contain its narrative to the sports page. It seems now that every time there are people on the march off the field of play, it finds an echo in the supposedly apolitical world of sport.

In October 2009, in the weeks before a 200,000-person protest for Lesbian, Gay, Bisexual, and Transgendered rights, two NFL players—Pro-Bowler Brendon Ayanbadejo and New Orleans Saints Super Bowl hero Scott Fujita—came out in favor of LGBT marriage equality. As Ayanbadejo said, "We will look back in ten, twenty, thirty years and be amazed that gays and lesbians did not have the same rights as everyone else."

This more recent political eruption is perhaps a hangover from the 2008 elections when an unprecedented number of athletes went public in support of Barack Obama's candidacy. NBA demigod LeBron James wore Obama T-shirts to games, and All-Star players like Baron Davis and Chauncey Billups also vocally supported the campaign. This was remarkable because some of the most commercially successful—and therefore some of the most commercially vulnerable—jocks became involved in the campaign. Boston Celtics star Kevin Garnett wore sneakers with "Vote for Change" scrawled on their sides. The Denver Nuggets' Carmelo Anthony pledged that he would score forty-four points in a game in honor of the future forty-fourth president (he only scored twenty-eight, which was, one can assume, not a tribute to Woodrow Wilson).

A new generation of "Jocks for Justice" is losing the yoke of apathy and speaking out about the world. NBA players like Steve Nash, Etan

Thomas, and Joakim Noah raised objections against the US war in Iraq. NFL players like Scott Fujita and Adalius Thomas did the same. Even Ultimate Fighting Champion Jeff "Snowman" Monson hands out antiwar pamphlets on his way to the "Octogon" and was out protesting at the 2008 Republican National Convention. As Martina Navratilova said to *Sports Illustrated* in 2008, "It's like athletes have woken up to what actors and musicians have known forever: I have this amazing platform—why not use it?"

These small acts of solidarity may seem negligible. But they matter. Whether we like it or not, whether we agree with it or not, athletes are role models. We can disagree and say that athletes shouldn't be cast in that role, but as the saying goes, you can disagree with gravity, but it won't help you if you're falling out of an airplane. Since athletes are role models, and since a microscopic fraction of young people will actually become pro players, it's worth asking the question: what are they modeling? It shouldn't just be the worst examples—like football player Ben Roethlisberger being investigated twice for rape or Donte Stallworth driving while intoxicated and killing a man with his car.

It's not every athlete who acts like their life's ambition off the court is to be featured on *MTV Cribs*. But if instead of modeling crass materialism, more athletes exemplify the idea that what you have to say is as important as what you can do on the court, then that can make a real difference. It also becomes a living expression that we have entered a new era.

The facts certainly say that more athletes are speaking out. But why is it happening over the last two years? One theory is that with the explosion of social media—especially Twitter—more athletes are seeing the value in going around the media filter and speaking their minds directly to fans. We've certainly seen this in the battle for collective bargaining agreements in the NFL and NBA as players use these technologies to express their opinions.

Another theory is that players are now actually encouraged for commercial reasons to "define their own brand." I spoke at a seminar for NBA rookies where the dominant theme was about advising players to distinguish themselves and create a memorable persona for NBA fans. Just repeating rote clichés like "we give 150 percent" and "play one game at a time" is now seen as a liability.

But the answer that makes the most sense is simply that athletes don't live on Planet Jock. They are part of this world and the level of crisis right now in the United States is something that has even breached the citadel of American sports. Recession. War. Immigrant-bashing. Oil spills. These are hardly the salad days. Jordan's ascendancy took place during the so-called vacation from history in the 1990s. Well, history has returned with a vengeance, severe enough to puncture the moated citadel of professional sports.

In March 2011, I asked Dr. Carlos for his thoughts about the protests in Wisconsin. "I don't think Governor Walker realizes that workers are the people who built this country," he said. "Workers are the people who keep the fabric of our communities together. Workers are the people of the grass roots. These workers in the public sector are also disproportionately African American. My mother, remember, was a nurse at Bellevue. For him or any political figure to try and cut their wages, take their health care, crush their unions, or subjugate them in any way is just a travesty. I commend what the workers, students, and all protesters are doing to stand up for their rights, and I am with them 1,000 percent. Every person from the world of sports with a heart or sense of humanity would say those words as well."

As a new generation of athletes and activists raises its fist, they can rest in the confidence that it's been done before. John Carlos dared and continues to dare to be more than just a brand. He has dared to live by a set of principles at great personal and professional cost. It's a standard we should all aspire toward . . . if we dare.

Appendix

■ ■ ■ ■

John W. Carlos's
Track and Field Records

compiled by Derek L. Toliver, Olympic track and field historian

San Jose State College

1969 NCAA All-American Team Honors

100-yard dash	9.2 seconds
220-yard dash	20.2 seconds
440-yard relay	39.1 seconds
60-yard dash	6.0 seconds

USA Track and Field Record-Breaking Performances

7 World Records, 8 American Records, 1 Olympic Record, 1 Pan Am Games, 2 NCAA, & 1 AAU Records

Statistics courtesy of the Journal of Olympic Track and Field Athletics, *www.olympictrack.org*

100-yard dash	9.1 seconds	Outdoors	Ties World Record & American Record	Fresno, CA	May 10, 1969
60-yard dash	5.9 seconds	Indoors	Ties **World Record** & American Record	College Park, MD	Jan. 10, 1969
60-yard dash	5.9 seconds	Indoors	Ties **World Record** & American Record	Baltimore, MD	Feb. 8, 1970
200-meter dash	19.7 seconds	Outdoors	Breaks **World Record** & American Record	Echo Summit, CA	Sept. 12, 1968
220-yard dash	21.2 seconds	Indoors	Breaks **World Record** & American Record *(220 yds timed en route to 300-yd time of 30.3)*	East Lansing, MI	Feb. 14, 1970
130-yard dash	11.7 seconds	Outdoors (grass)	Breaks **World Record** & American Record	Melbourne, Australia	Mar. 17, 1970
200-meter dash	20.11 seconds	Outdoors	Breaks Olympic Record *(Set in the semifinals from Lane 1)*	Mexico City Olympic Games	Oct. 16, 1968
440-yard relay	38.8 seconds	Outdoors	Breaks American Record	Knoxville, TN NCAA Championship	June 20, 1969
220-yard dash	20.2 seconds	Outdoors	Ties NCAA Championship Meet Record	Knoxville, TN	June 21, 1969
220-yard dash	20.2 seconds	Outdoors	Breaks AAU Championship Meet Record	Miami, FL	June 29, 1969
60-yard dash	6.0 seconds	Indoors	Ties NCAA Meet Record	Detroit, MI	May 15, 1969
200-meter dash	20.5 seconds	Outdoors	Breaks Pan Am Games Record	Winnipeg, Canada	Aug. 2, 1967
70-meter dash	7.3 seconds	Indoors	Breaks **World Record** & American Record *(set as a professional on the ITA* circuit)*	Pocatello, ID	Feb. 24, 1974

* *ITA stands for the Professional International Track Association.*

Establishes First NCAA Sprint Grand Slam*

1969 NCAA Outdoor Championship	100-yard dash	9.2 seconds
1969 NCAA Outdoor Championship	220-yard dash	20.2 seconds
1969 NCAA Outdoor Championship	440-yard relay	39.1 seconds
1969 NCAA Indoor Championship	60-yard dash	6.0 seconds

John W. Carlos, running for San Jose State College, is the only sprinter in NCAA history to accomplish the NCAA Sprint Grand Slam, winning the four above races in the calendar year. The term, "NCAA Sprint Grand Slam" was created by Derek L. Toliver, editor and publisher of the Journal of Track and Field Athletics.

Runs Fastest 100m and 200m One-Day Performance in History

John W. Carlos was the first man in world history to run 100 meters in sub 9.9 and 200 meters in 20.0 on the same day at the Indian Summer Games in So. Lake Tahoe, CA, on September 12, 1969

100-meter dash outdoors	9.9	1st Place
200-meter dash outdoors	20.0	1st Place

Becomes the First Sprinter in History
to Hold Concurrent World Records in 60 Yard
and 220 Yard

John W. Carlos is the only sprinter in world history to hold concurrent world records in the following sprint events: Indoor 60-yard or 60-meter dash, Indoor 220-yard or 200-meter dash, Outdoor 100-yard or 100-meter dash, Outdoor 220 yards or 200 meters

Indoor 60-yard dash	5.9 seconds	1969
Indoor 60-yard dash (WR set in Heats)	5.9 seconds	1970
Indoor 220-yard dash (timed at 220 yds en route to 300 yd at 30.3)	21.2 seconds	1970
Indoor 70-meter dash (Pro ITA* circuit)	7.3 seconds	1974
Outdoor 100-yard dash	9.1 seconds	1969
Outdoor 200-meter dash	19.7† seconds	1968
Outdoor 130-yard dash (grass track)	11.7 seconds	1970

* ITA stands for the Professional International Track Association.

† The Olympic Shoe Wars between Rivals Puma and Adidas may have cost John W. Carlos his 19.7 second 200-meter world record: The 19.7-second 200-meter dash world record was never ratified by the International Amateur Athletic Federation (IAAF) due to the new 68–brush spike configuration on the shoes worn by John W. Carlos. The previously approved shoe spike configuration was a long four- to six-spike shoe. Many track and field experts felt the failure to ratify record by the IAAF was a result of the "Shoe Wars" between the rival Puma and Adidas athletic shoe companies. Adidas had recently won the 1968 Olympic sponsorship. It is unfortunate that the 200-meter world record set by John W. Carlos may never be ratified due to the ongoing competitive battle between the rival shoe companies (both owned by the Dassler brothers). The Dassler brothers were the original founding partners of Adidas before one left Adidas to form the rival Puma Shoe Company. Source: Journal of Track & Field Athletics

Seven World Records
and Lifetime Best Marks by Event

100-yard dash	9.0 wind-aided (outdoors)	Wind-aided but first man in history to run 9.0 seconds under any conditions	San Jose, CA	1969
100-yard dash	9.1 legal (outdoors)	Tied world record	Fresno, CA	1969
100-meter dash	9.9 wind-aided (outdoors)	Wind-aided, over legal wind limit for world record		1969
100-meter dash	10.0 legal (outdoors)	Tied second fastest time in history	So. Lake Tahoe	1968
220-yard dash	20.2 legal (outdoors)	Tied NCAA Champ Meet record	Knoxville, TN	1969
220-yard dash	20.2 legal (outdoors)	Tied AAU Champ Meet record	Miami, FL	1970
200-meter dash	19.7 legal (outdoors)	Broke world record	So. Lake Tahoe	1968
60-yard dash	5.9 (indoors)	Tied world record	College Park, MD	1969
60-yard dash	5.9 (indoors)	Tied world record	Baltimore, MD	1970
220-yard dash	21.2 (indoors)	Broke world record	East Lansing, MI	1970
130-yard dash	11.7 (outdoors)	Broke world record	Melbourne, Australia	1970
70-meter dash	7.3 (indoors)	Broke world record (*pro ITA* circuit*)	Pocatello, ID	1974

* ITA stands for the Professional International Track Association.

John W. Carlos, USA & San Jose State College, burns 100 yards in record 9.1, windy 9.0 second 100 meters in 10.1, and windy 9.9 and 220 yards in 20.2 and 200 meters in 20.0. He ran the fastest 220-yard race ever recorded in the east with a 20.2 in Miami, FL

Distance	Place	Location/Event	Date	Distance	Place	Location/Event	Date
9.5 yards	1	Dogwood Relays	Apr. 19, 1969	20.4 yards	1	San Jose	Mar. 29, 1969
9.2 yards	1	Mt. SAC Relays	Apr. 26, 1969	20.3 yards	1	King Games	May 18, 1969
9.0 yards	1	San Jose	May 3, 1969	20.4 yards	1	Calif Relays	May 24, 1969
9.1 yards	1	W. Coast Relays	May 10, 1969	20.7 yards	1	Colise-Compton	June 7, 1969
10.1 meters	1	King Games	May 18, 1969	20.4 yards	1	NCAA - Heats	June 19, 1969
10.1 meters	1	Calif. Relays	May 24, 1969	20.2 yards	1	NCAA - Final	June 21, 1969
9.5 yards	1	Colise-Compton	June 7, 1969	20.3 yards	1	AAU - Heats	June 29, 1969
9.3 yards	1	NCAA - Heats	June 19, 1969	20.2 yards	1	AAU - Final	June 29, 1969
9.1 yards	1	NCAA - Semis	June 20, 1969	20.8 yards	1	Dayton	July 5, 1969
9.2 yards	1	NCAA - Final	June 20, 1969	21.3 yards	1	Honolulu	July 12, 1969
9.3 yards	1	AAU - Heat	June 28, 1969	20.3 meters	1	US vs. USSR/BC	July 19, 1969
9.3 yards	2	AAU - Final	June 28, 1969	20.4 meters	1	US vs. Euro	July 31, 1969
9.4 yards	1	Honolulu	July 12, 1969	20.3 meters	1	US vs. W. Germany	Aug. 6, 1969
10.3 meters	1	USA vs. USSR/BC	July 18, 1969	20.0 meters	1	Indian Summer	Sept. 12, 1969
10.3 meters	1	Malmo Sweden	July 24, 1969				
10.2 meters	1	US vs. Europe	July 30, 1969				
10.1 meters	1	US vs. W. Germany	Aug. 5, 1969				
9.9 meters	1	Indian Summer	Sept. 12, 1969				

Worldwide coverge of track and field, 1969 annual edition, Track and Field, *vol. 22, no. 18, January 1970.*

John W. Carlos, USA & Seamans International, won with a legal 9.2 second 100-yard dash, tying the fastest time ever recorded on the East Coast above the Mason-Dixon line (set at the 1970 Penn Relays). He ran 100 meters in 10.1 legal and 10.0 windy. He turned in his second consecutive undefeated season in the furlong with best times of 20.3 for 220 yards and 20.2 for 200 meters.

Distance	Place	Location/Event	Date	Distance	Place	Location/Event	Date
9.4 yards	1	San Jose	Mar. 7, 1970	20.8 yards	1	San Jose	Mar. 7, 1970
11.7 - 130 yards	1	Melbourne, Australia World Record	Mar. 17, 1970	20.3 yards	1	Melbourne, Aus	Mar. 17, 1970
9.3 yards	1	San Jose	Apr. 4, 1970	20.8 yards	1	San Jose	Apr. 7, 1970
9.3 yards	1	Kansas Relays	Apr. 18, 1970	20.3 yards	1	San Jose	May 2, 1970
9.2 yards	1	Penn Relays	Apr. 25, 1970	20.4 meters	1	King Games	May 16, 1970
10.1 meters	1	King Games	May 16, 1970	20.6 yards	1	California Relays	May 23, 1970
10.0 meters	1	California Relays	May 23, 1970	20.4 yards	1	Kennedy Games	May 30, 1970
9.4 yards	1	Kennedy Games	May 30, 1970	20.8 yards	1	Compton Invitation	June 6, 1970
9.5 yards	1	Compton Invitation	June 6, 1970	20.4 yards	1	Rose Festival	June 13, 1970
9.4 yards	1	Rose Festival	June 13, 1970	20.4 yards	1	Orange Invitational	June 20, 1970
9.3 yards	1	Orange Invitation	June 20, 1970				
No Time	9	AAU - Injured	June 26, 1970				

John W. Carlos, running for San Jose State College, won 3 Individual, 1 Relay, and (1) Team NCAA Championship titles during the 1969 season. Here are his record 5 NCAA Championship performances during the 1969 season

60-yard dash*	6.0 finals	1st Place	NCAA Champion & NCAA Meet Record	Detroit, MI	March 15, 1969
100-yard dash*	9.2 finals	1st Place Champion	NCAA Champion	Knoxville, TN	June 20, 1969
100-yard dash	9.1 semifinals	1st Place	Ties World Record but, Wind-aided	Knoxville, TN	June 20, 1969
220-yard dash†	20.2 finals	1st Place	NCAA Champion & NCAA Meet Record	Knoxville, TN	June 21, 1969
440-yard relay†	39.1 finals	1st Place	NCAA Champion	Knoxville, TN	June 21, 1969
440-yard relay	38.8 semifinals	1st Place	American Record	Knoxville, TN	June 20, 1969
1969 NCAA Team Championship*	48 points for San Jose State	1st Place	NCAA Team Championship	Knoxville, TN	June 21, 1969
220-yard dash	20.2 finals	1st Place	AAU Champion & AAU Meet Record	Miami, FL	June 29, 1969
100-yard dash	9.3 finals	2nd Place	AAU Runner-up	Miami, FL	June 28, 1969

* *Track and Field News*, "The Bible of the Sport," recognized John W. Carlos as the "World's Fastest Sprinter" in both 1969 and 1970. He was also recognized by *Track and Field News* as the World's Number One Runner in 1969. This made John W. Carlos the "World's Fastest Human" in both 1969 and 1970. It is very rare for any sprinter to be ranked number one in the world in both the 100y/100m and 20y/200m for two consecutive years. In fifty-two outdoor final races from 1969 to 1970, he only lost two races and they were at the 100y/100m distances (lost to Ivory Crockett at the 1969 AAU Championships where both men timed in 9.3 and lost to Charlie Greene at the Dr. King Games in 1969 where both men clocked 10.1).

World's Fastest Human Indoors 50-Yard Dash
to 300-Yard Dash in 1969 and 1970

John W. Carlos set three indoor world records: two at 60 yards and one at 220 yards. He was also generally unbeatable at 300 yards indoors and threatened to break that record quite often winning the 50-yard or 60-yard dash and then winning the 300-yard dash in the same meet. It is rare to find a sprinter who is quick enough out of the starting block to set a world record at 60 yards, and strong enough to have the endurance to run 300 yards at near world record pace. Most sprinters have one or the other and not both speed and endurance.

Here are the world rankings for John W. Carlos as complied by *Track & Field News*:

Year	100 yd / 100 meter	220 yd / 200 meter
1967	Unranked	3rd
1968	Unranked	3rd
1969	1st	1st
1970	1st	1st

About Haymarket Books

Haymarket Books is a nonprofit, progressive book distributor and publisher, a project of the Center for Economic Research and Social Change. We believe that activists need to take ideas, history, and politics into the many struggles for social justice today. Learning the lessons of past victories, as well as defeats, can arm a new generation of fighters for a better world. As Karl Marx said, "The philosophers have merely interpreted the world; the point however is to change it."

We take inspiration and courage from our namesakes, the Haymarket Martyrs, who gave their lives fighting for a better world. Their 1886 struggle for the eight-hour day reminds workers around the world that ordinary people can organize and struggle for their own liberation.

For more information and to shop our complete catalog of titles, visit us online at www.haymarketbooks.org.

Also from Haymarket Books

What's My Name, Fool?: Sports and Resistance in the United States
Dave Zirin

Welcome to the Terrordome: The Pain, Politics, and Promise of Sports
Dave Zirin, foreword by Chuck D

Floodlines: Community and Resistance from Katrina to the Jena Six
Jordan Flaherty

Palante: Young Lords Party
Text by Young Lords Party, photographs by Michael Abramson,
foreword by Iris Morales

Black Liberation and Socialism
Ahmed Shawki

*People Wasn't Made to Burn: A True Story of Race, Murder,
and Justice in Chicago*, Joe Allen